Deconstructing
Reagan

Deconstructing Reagan

Conservative Mythology and America's Fortieth President

Kyle Longley • Jeremy D. Mayer
Michael Schaller • John W. Sloan

Routledge
Taylor & Francis Group

LONDON AND NEW YORK

First published 2007 by M.E. Sharpe

Published 2015 by Routledge
2 Park Square, Milton Park, Abingdon, Oxon OX14 4RN
711 Third Avenue, New York, NY 10017, USA

Routledge is an imprint of the Taylor & Francis Group, an informa business

Library of Congress Cataloging-in-Publication Data

Deconstructing Reagan : conservative mythology and America's fortieth president /
Kyle Longley . . . [et al.].
   p. cm.
Includes bibliographical references and index.
ISBN 13: 978-0-7656-1590-9 (cloth : alk. paper)
ISBN 10: 0-7656-1590-8 (cloth : alk. paper)
  1. Reagan, Ronald—Influence. 2. Reagan, Ronald—Public opinion. 3. Conservatism—
United States. 4. Symbolism in politics—United States. 5. United States—Politics and
government—1981–1989. 6. United States—Politics and government—1945–1989.
7. United States—Politics and government—1989– 8. Public opinion—United States.
I. Longley, Kyle.

E877.2.D44 2007
973.927092—dc22   2006016005

ISBN 13: 9780765615916 (pbk)
ISBN 13: 9780765615909 (hbk)

Contents

Introduction

American Conservatism

Am I big enough man for the race?
—*Warren G. Harding*

Don't make me laugh! The day of giants in the Presidential chair is
past. Our so-called Great Presidents were all made by the conditions
of war under which they administered the office. Greatness in the
Presidential chair is largely an illusion of the people.
—*Harry M. Daugherty, The Inside Story of the Harding Tragedy*

In February 1999, Republican congressman Matt Salmon from Arizona
defended his recent legislative proposal that called for putting Ronald
Reagan's face on Mount Rushmore. According to Salmon, Reagan was
an outstanding president for several reasons. "Reagan won the Cold
War without firing a shot," he stressed, "making him one of the greatest
presidents." In addition, Reagan "inaugurated the unprecedented economic growth we have been enjoying now for 17 years, and he restored
America's hope and faith in the future." Salmon complained bitterly
about President Bill Clinton's "outrageous conduct" and stated, "Our
children should be discussing the achievements of other presidents."
"Once upon a time, Ronald Reagan brought America back from 'malaise,'" he emphasized, adding, "Perhaps through this debate, the Gipper
can bring America back again, this time from the destructive cynicism
sweeping our nation."[1]

It was not surprising that Salmon would propose what one constituent
characterized as an "ill-conceived publicity stunt" that captured national
media coverage, including discussion on the *Today* show. Salmon was a
classic Reagan supporter, a white male in his mid-forties, comparatively
affluent, and a religious fundamentalist from the state that produced Barry
Goldwater, not far from the hotbed of Reagan conservatism, southern
California. He had a record of fierce partisanship and voted for limited
government with the exception of intervention into people's private

lives regarding abortion and homosexuality. He also wanted to position himself as he left Congress for a run for Arizona governor in 2002, in which he knew he would face in the primary several potentially strong Republican challengers with moderate credentials. He clearly calculated the Mount Rushmore maneuver to gain support among conservative voters in Arizona.

While Salmon's legislation never went anywhere, there are many examples of efforts by conservatives to promote their hero, Ronald Reagan, and by extension the conservative movement. Their labors have been impressive. A special commission, the Ronald Reagan Legacy Project, whose national advisory board members included Karl Rove and John Ashcroft, evolved to make sure that every county in the United States has a statue or another type of memorial to Reagan. Each year conservatives push for more buildings, airports, schools, and streets to be named after the former president. There are already many instances including the National Airport, the Department of Commerce building, and an aircraft carrier.

The Republicans' euphoria after the elections in 2000 and 2002 when they took control of the executive and legislative branches ensured even more efforts to enshrine Reagan in the American political pantheon. Some legislators even proposed building a memorial on the Washington mall, although Reagan had signed a bill that prohibited such action until twenty-five years after the person's death. Yet they sought an exemption. Others called for replacing Franklin Roosevelt's face on the dime or, at the least, minting half with Reagan's portrait. Some legislators even proposed replacing founding father Alexander Hamilton on the $10 bill. The mobilization also included driving a biopic that was perceived as negative off mainstream television and the second Bush administration's executive order stopping the release of Reagan-era government documents, in part to shield the former president from scrutiny.[2]

The intent is clear from statements of those doing a significant amount of the work. Grover Norquist of Americans for Tax Reform emphasized that renaming the National Airport allowed for "100,000 mini-civics lessons" for the small children flying into Reagan National Airport. A new generation would ask questions about Reagan, and parents would have the opportunity to tell about his rising from humble beginnings to become a great president, all the while stressing the conservative values that he represented.[3]

Norquist answers a large question: why some prominent conservatives rush forward to idolize Reagan as well as the efforts of those like Salmon. The most important reason is that they need a hero to perpetuate their political vision and win contemporary support. They need symbols to elicit fond memories of their political movement. Politics is often about symbolism and being able to find a common positive image to stir emotion. This need has been a long-term component of American politics. This is especially true in the efforts to win middle America, both in the struggle for control between progressives, moderates, and conservatives within the Republican Party and in general elections against the Democrats. The politics of symbolism is an important component of any political movement.[4]

The major question that must be addressed is why conservatives have latched onto Reagan and so desperately tried to enshrine him within the pantheon of American leaders. The major reason is that they have few alternatives at a national level. In the twentieth century, conservatives have primarily allied with the Republican Party except for southern Democrats, who eventually bolted the Democratic Party and merged with the Republicans in the 1950s and 1960s in response to civil rights and cultural issues. As a result of that change, the traditional political icon of the Republican Party, Abraham Lincoln, became much less palatable to political leaders and the rank and file in the South. While many uphold Lincoln within the party, especially outside of the South and Mountain West, his status clearly has suffered over time.

The best-known Republican president of the early twentieth century was Theodore Roosevelt. However, he presents few palatable ideas to conservatives. He battled big business, supported conservation efforts, and actively involved the United States in world affairs, often in areas not considered of vital interest to the United States. Furthermore, he broke from the Republican Party in 1912 and formed the Bull Moose Party, which many believed handed the presidency to Democrat Woodrow Wilson. Clearly, Roosevelt was too moderate and progressive for conservatives.

The only real conservative of the first half of the twentieth century was one of Reagan's heroes, Calvin Coolidge. He favored big business, stating that the "business of America is business." His hands-off style of management, anticommunism, and willingness to defer to Secretary of the Treasury Andrew Mellon, who pushed huge tax cuts for the wealthy, made Coolidge a prime candidate. Several obstacles existed, however. First, Coolidge lacked charisma and inspired few outside the ranks of dedicated and educated conservatives. More important, a whole generation of Americans saw him as largely contributing to the onset of the Great Depression, thus dooming his entry into the political pantheon.

The conservatives of the 1930s and 1940s found themselves under the heel of the Great Depression and the New Deal and the popularity of Franklin Roosevelt. At about the time they found themselves on the upswing at the end of the 1930s, World War II intervened and the identification with isolationism undermined their appeal. Furthermore, within that period, moderate Republicans led by Wendell Willkie and Thomas Dewey took leadership roles.

In the postwar era, as Truman and the Democratic Party lost ground and the conservatives appeared on the verge of seizing control of the Republican Party under the leadership of Robert Taft, Joseph McCarthy, and William Knowland, a new, moderate force in the Republican Party, General Dwight Eisenhower, co-opted them. The first Republican president since 1933, Eisenhower believed in specific parts of early conservative orthodoxy, especially the emphasis on a balanced budget. Yet he did little to roll back the popular New Deal programs and actually expanded government's role in building federal highways and funding education. He also provided some support for civil rights, including the use of federal troops to enforce a desegregation order in Little Rock, Arkansas.

In foreign policy, Eisenhower was a strong anticommunist, but not to the degree favored by many rabid anticommunist conservatives. He opposed the witch-hunts conducted by McCarthy, ultimately helping ensure the Wisconsin senator's demise. Also, he negotiated with the Soviets on nuclear testing, a sure sign of weakness in many conservatives' eyes. Eisenhower also would warn about the development of the "military-industrial" complex, another indication of unwillingness to pay the necessary price. Furthermore, Eisenhower opposed attempts to rein in the power of the executive by his strong opposition to the Bricker Amendment, which would have limited the ability of the president to join foreign alliances without congressional approval.

Finally, Eisenhower believed that right-wing conservatives were a divisive, corrosive force in American politics. He described them as "the most ignorant people living in the United States," adding in 1956 that "I think far from appeasing or reasoning with the dyed-in-the-wool reactionary fringe, we should completely ignore it, and when necessary, repudiate it."[5] Such attitudes, many published from personal diaries after he left the White House, have made him very unpopular with many conservatives, although moderate Republicans rallied to his side.

For many modern conservatives, Barry Goldwater was the founder of their movement. They liked his appeal to limited government, including opposition to civil rights and many government health and education programs. The Arizonan's bold statements, such as "extremism in the defense of liberty is no vice. And . . . moderation in the pursuit of justice is no virtue," heartened many conservatives. His ardent anticommunism and willingness to give army commanders discretionary authority for the use of tactical nuclear weapons emboldened those who wanted a president tough on Moscow.[6]

Goldwater had two major strikes against him in efforts to fully enshrine him in the political pantheon, especially among middle Americans, who often viewed him as an extremist. First, he lost the presidential election by a huge margin to Lyndon Johnson. Johnson took over 61 percent of the popular vote and won the electoral vote, 486 to 52. Goldwater took only his home state, Louisiana, Mississippi, Alabama, Georgia, and South Carolina. While some argue that he lost in defense of principle, he still suffered a substantial defeat, limiting his access to political stardom. Most Americans like and remember winners.

More important, Goldwater never adopted fully the principles of contemporary conservative orthodoxy. He never was a social conservative and remained consistently opposed to government interference in private matters. His first wife Peggy was a founding member of Planned Parenthood in Arizona, and he never made *Roe v. Wade* a cornerstone of his principles. When Christian evangelist Jerry Falwell denounced the 1981 nomination of Sandra Day O'Connor to the Supreme Court because she lacked antiabortion credentials, Goldwater called on every "good Christian . . . to kick Jerry Falwell right in the ass."[7]

Goldwater also failed another litmus test among social conservatives over homosexuality. Never a religious fundamentalist or cultural warrior, he said in 1994 that he supported gays in the military: "You don't need to be straight to fight and die for your country. You just need to shoot straight."[8] While many conservatives argued that Goldwater's second wife Susan corrupted him with her ideas, they ignore that throughout his life he was a conservative with civil libertarian leanings in all areas of life.

Still another action isolated Goldwater from conservatives. Violating a fundamental Reagan principle, he criticized his fellow Republican, Governor Fife Symington. At several junctures in his career, he supported Democratic candidates Dennis DeConcini and Mo Udall over Republican ones when he believed the opposition party member was better. He even contributed money to Democratic candidates. For him, partisanship had a place, but not at the expense of the country. This stance further isolated him from those who choose who sits in the pantheon of conservative heroes.

For his transgressions, at times, Goldwater received the wrath of conservatives. In 1994, conservative Republicans tried to remove his name from the state party headquarters named after him, calling Goldwater "an embarrassment" who sounded like he had "lost it." Others protested his positions, and he does not figure as prominently in conservative lore in Arizona as Reagan, whom some legislators tried to honor by creating a special license plate. Goldwater never seemed to mind. When asked about the criticisms, he simply replied, "You know something, I don't give a damn."[9]

The next in line to inherit the conservative mantle after Goldwater should have been Richard Nixon. The rabid anticommunist who helped McCarthy appeared likely to roll back the Great Society tide. Yet conservatives never really liked Nixon for several reasons. First, by supporting the creation of the Environmental Protection Agency and extending affirmative action through executive order, he did not show proper dedication to conservative causes.

Most important, Nixon did the unthinkable in foreign policy. He negotiated with the Soviets over various issues, including disarmament, in what his administration called détente. Even more sinister, Nixon opened relations with the communist government of China. Through secret negotiations, he helped push along the process of normalization of relations, in turn moving the United States away from its full commitment to Taiwan as the legitimate government of China. On its own, each of these actions would have doomed him among conservatives, but taken together they bordered on treason to some, especially those within the China Lobby.

Finally, Nixon disqualified himself with his actions. The numerous underhanded activities related to foreign policy and reelection that ultimately concluded in Watergate and his resignation in disgrace alienated even his most ardent supporters. How could conservatives uphold Nixon as a hero when the majority of Americans viewed him as a contemptible crook? Fortunately for conservatives of all persuasions, not long after, Reagan became the standard-bearer of their movement.

After Reagan, entry into the conservative pantheon became even more difficult as he cast a long shadow. George H.W. Bush, who had languished in Reagan's shadow throughout the 1980s, won the presidency, but not really conservative support. His moderate positions on abortion and other cultural issues, his commitment to negotiate with the Soviet Union and perceived proxies elsewhere, and his famous commitment to "read my lips, no new taxes," a pact he violated, led to significant conservative antipathy. As one commentator lamented, Bush's "failure demonstrated the truth of the maxim that you can take the country-club Republican out of the golf course, but you cannot take the golf course out of the Republican."[10]

That left Reagan as the sole standard-bearer of the conservative movement until the rise of George W. Bush. Dinesh D'Souza stresses that "Reagan was not merely a successful president who belongs in the impressive corner of Woodrow Wilson, Harry Truman, and Dwight Eisenhower, Reagan was truly a great president whose achievement rivals that of Franklin Roosevelt. Only the two nation builders, Washington and Lincoln, occupy a more elevated place in the presidential pantheon."[11]

D'Souza melds the two approaches to the memory of Reagan. On one hand, there are those who truly struggle to maintain Reagan's legacy because of their devotion to the president. There is some precedent for this approach. In John Kennedy's case, people such as his advisers Arthur Schlesinger Jr. and Theodore Sorenson sought to sustain a vision of Camelot built on the legacy of the president and not necessarily an ideology. In Reagan's case, this personal approach is seen in the works of family and close associates such as Nancy Reagan, Michael Deaver, Peter Wallison, Martin Anderson, and Kiron Skinner, the editor of his diaries and letters. They are the guardians of the memory of Reagan and his legacies, and they push hard to portray him through the prism of their devotion.[12]

However, many pushing to memorialize Reagan have, besides a commitment to the president, their own political agenda as a driving force. They understand the symbolic value of Reagan in winning the struggle for the hearts and minds of middle America as well as shoring up their standing among the Republican base. Conservatives want to convince Americans that Reagan was a hero and that, since he represents their values, they should have political power. He put a "kinder, gentler" face on the conservative movement, whose leaders have included Republican politicians Strom Thurmond, Robert Taft, William Knowland, Jesse Helms, Newt Gingrich, Trent Lott, Pat Robertson, Pat Buchanan, Dan Burton, Tom DeLay, and their supporters, such as

Conservative activists Rupert Murdoch, Richard Mellon Scaife, Rush Limbaugh, James Dobson, and Oliver North. In each case, these people have typically appealed to the conservative base, but they have little reach beyond because of their polarizing nature and middle America's negative perceptions of them. While the conservative label has not become politically radioactive, like the liberal one, it has often been viewed as reactionary, racist, xenophobic, and elitist by its opponents and some middle Americans. This is why Senator James Jeffords of Vermont, for example, found living within a party that kowtowed to the extreme fringe so disconcerting that he decided to become an independent in 2001. Therefore, having Reagan as a conservative icon, one with much higher approval ratings among the general public, makes the task much easier than harkening back to Thurmond, Taft, or others. As the *Wall Street Journal* observed, Reagan shifted conservatism from the cranky opposition to a self-confident ruling philosophy: "Pre-Reagan, 20th-century American conservatism had been tinged with gloominess: Western civilization was in decline and the road to serfdom inevitable. Mr. Reagan never signed on. Unlike some on the right (and almost all on the left), he had a deeper faith both in American principles and in a human nature that owed itself to a Divine hand that had made men free and made America to prove it."[13]

This change largely explains the rush to memorialize Reagan as conservatives understand the importance of symbolism in American politics, especially in a struggle for legitimacy in middle America. In part, this is why Senator Sam Brownback of Kansas, a presidential candidate for 2008, can stand up in front of a large crowd and crow, "I am Sam Brownback and I am a Ronald Reagan Republican."[14] That is why Matt Salmon pushed for putting Reagan's face on Mount Rushmore in 1999, and it helps explain many of the other efforts to memorialize Reagan.

It should also be noted that there are those who are fearful of such actions going overboard. Some conservatives believe that the efforts to mythologize Reagan have gone too far. Reagan's biographer, Lou Cannon, believes that Reagan "would have been very uneasy about this. They're doing something Reagan himself would not have wanted done, and they're doing something that is unnecessary. The conservative movement may be in trouble, but I don't think Reagan's reputation is." Conservative columnist George Will agrees that there is "something un-Reaganesque about trying to plaster his name all over the country the way Lenin was plastered over Eastern Europe, Mao over China and Saddam Hussein all over Iraq. It's time for us to rescue Ronald Reagan and his legacy from his more zealous friends."[15]

Nevertheless, as Matt Salmon's statements demonstrate, several cornerstones of the conservative mythology surrounding Reagan stand out and as a result deserve special attention. These include Reagan's role in winning the Cold War and the long-term impact of his foreign policy, Reagan's economic policy and whether it really laid the groundwork for the growth of the 1990s, Reagan's representation of the common people in his rhetoric and actions, and finally the character issue that entered the debate during the Clinton presidency.

The essays contained in this book seek to add a level of debate to the arguments of conservatives regarding the Reagan presidency. Each raises the question of the convergence of myth and reality and critically analyzes various parts of the standard arguments for the greatness of Ronald Reagan. The goal is to provoke thought and debate, thereby achieving the kind of balanced and rational approach that often has been absent in examinations of the Reagan presidency, as those who admired or despised him have dominated the debate.

The first essay focuses on issues related to Reagan's foreign policy and its short- and long-term consequences, with particular attention to the argument that Reagan won the Cold War. Professor Michael Schaller, Regent's Professor at the University of Arizona, builds on his substantial work on Reagan in books, including *Right Turn: American Life in the Reagan-Bush Era, 1980–1992* (2006) and *Reckoning with Reagan: America and Its President in the 1980s* (1992) to question "whether arms spending and tough talk had much to do with changing Soviet policy." While acknowledging that Reagan had a role in the collapse of the USSR, Schaller examines other factors, including Mikhail Gorbachev and internal Soviet weaknesses. In addition, in order to place Reagan's legacy in a larger context, he looks at the role of Reagan in the nonindustrialized world and the long-term impact of supporting the Muslim fighters in Afghanistan as well as the U.S. buildup of Saddam Hussein in Iraq and its ultimate results.

The second essay, by John W. Sloan of the Political Science Department of the University of Houston, builds on his earlier work, *The Reagan Effect: Economics and Presidential Leadership* (1999). Sloan argues that the Reagan administration "did succeed—partly by design, partly by compromise, partly by muddling through—in creating a conservative regime that was capable of promoting long-term economic growth with low inflation." He examines the effect of tax cuts (and tax increases) on the economy as well as deficits, the significance of the Federal Reserve Board, and other important factors in order to understand the true impact of the Reagan administration's economic policies on the growth of the 1980s and 1990s.

In the third essay, Jeremy Mayer builds on the research in his book, *Running on Race: Racial Politics in Presidential Politics, 1960–2000* (2002). An assistant professor in the School of Public Policy at George Mason University, Mayer questions the basic idea that Reagan was a president for all Americans, an ordinary American who rose to become an extraordinary president. In particular, he focuses on the disconnect between Reagan and the African-American community. He emphasizes, "There are reasons why white America and black America perceived Reagan so differently." Mayer looks at Reagan's background, his rhetoric and actions, and the ultimate impact of the president's policies to answer the question of why the divide existed.

Finally, I focus on the issue of Reagan's character, building on my books, *In the Eagle's Shadow: The United States and Latin America* (2002) and a recent biography, *Senator Albert Gore, Sr.: Tennessee Maverick* (2004), which covered much of twentieth-century American politics. The essay asks questions about Reagan's character. It concentrates on the method of comparison, focusing on a character debate centered not on Bill Clinton, but on Jimmy Carter. It also looks at the differences between Reagan's rhetoric and actions on abortion and reviews the corruption and scandal that surrounded Reagan to contextualize his character. Finally, it addresses the perceptions created by Reagan's supporters, such as Peggy Noonan, and tests them against realities.

All these issues are important because the current administration of George W. Bush has vigorously tried to use the Reagan record to justify its actions, from high deficits to foreign military adventures. It is also likely that future conservatives will base their appeals on similar assertions. However, differences between the two presidencies abound, from comparing the struggle against the Soviet Union to the highly ambiguous, nebulous struggle against Muslim terrorism, the contrast between a $2 trillion debt and an $8 trillion (and rising) one, and the difference between Reagan's conservatism to Bush's "compassionate conservatism." Given the importance of the mythology, current policy makers and voters need to examine the realities before crafting public policy.

Even more important, there is the truth factor. Each essay asks important questions about determining the real Reagan legacy. Hopefully, in today's political culture, Americans will not digress to the level highlighted in the famous 1962 John Ford movie, *The Man Who Shot Liberty Valance.* At the end of the film, one of the main characters, Ransom Stoddard, asks the journalist covering the story, "You're not going to use the story, Mr. Scott?" Maxwell Scott replies, "This is the West, sir. When the legend becomes fact, print the legend."[16]

Deconstructing
Reagan

1

Reagan and the Cold War

Michael Schaller

Popular memories of Ronald Reagan focus on his embrace of free markets at home and strident anticommunism abroad. To many Americans, his unapologetic celebration of patriotism and military fortitude not only made the nation safer, but also in the words of British prime minister Margaret Thatcher, won the Cold War "without firing a shot." Upon his death in June 2004, Republican leaders such as Texas congressman Tom DeLay praised Reagan in a way few anticipated: as an "intellectual warrior" who "marshaled ideas like troops" and freed the world from the threat of communism. By then, Reagan had nearly passed into mythology. His once ridiculed naiveté was recalled as sincerity; his reputed laziness came to symbolize an inner calm; his well-known disinterest in details merely proved his mastery of the big picture.

Many of those who served the president, along with conservative journalists, praise his record of achievement. Shortly before Reagan left office in 1989, Robert McFarlane, the third of Reagan's six national security advisers, wrote his former boss that the transformation of the Soviet system represented a "vindication of your seven-year strategy." Confronted by the "renewal" of American economic, military, and spiritual power, Soviet leaders understood that "they simply had to change their system or face inevitable decline." One adoring chronicler, Peter Schweizer, argued the point more forcefully. Unlike presidents before him, Reagan made the roll back and defeat of communism a primary goal. Dwight D. Eisenhower and Richard M. Nixon talked a tough game, but valued stability over confrontation and sought to make deals with the Kremlin. Reagan, in contrast, considered communism both a moral evil and an

3

inherent threat to peace. By not only *talking* but also *acting* tough, by rearming America and challenging Soviet power globally, the "so-called bumpkin," as Schweizer put it admiringly, "won the cold war." Perhaps the shrillest praise of Reagan's foreign policy accomplishments came from journalist Ann Coulter. Liberals, she wrote, "lie about Reagan's victory because when Reagan won the Cold War, he proved them wrong on everything they had done and said throughout the Cold War. It is their last defense to fifty years of treason."[1]

Without question, Reagan expanded U.S. military power and restored public confidence in presidential leadership. His rhetoric stirred and lifted the spirits of Americans—and many foreigners—who had considered themselves victims in an unfriendly world of hostage taking, nuclear threats, rising oil prices, and third world insurgencies. Yet, as in his domestic policy, a gulf often existed between the idealism, self-assurance, and occasional bluster of Reagan's calls to action and his administration's actual accomplishments. To be sure, Reagan oversaw the largest military buildup in peacetime history and played a critical role in transforming the Soviet-American relationship. Whether arms spending and tough talk had much to do with changing Soviet policy remains uncertain. Other Reagan initiatives, such as using covert force in Central America, the Middle East, and Africa, had unintended, sometimes dire, consequences. U.S. intervention did not cause the violence endemic to these regions, but it did little to alleviate it or to further American interests. For example, the extensive program of the Central Intelligence Agency (CIA) from 1982 to 1988 of arming Islamist fighters resisting Soviet forces in Afghanistan ultimately promoted the rise of a fundamentalist terror network led by Osama bin Laden. Reagan's occasional support for dictatorships, along with a willingness to negotiate secretly with terrorists, marked some of his administration's worst failures. Reagan's penchant for unilateral military action still echoes in post–9/11 American foreign policy and is often cited by President George W. Bush and his aides as justification for some of their policies.

Background

Long after he rejected Franklin Roosevelt's New Deal liberalism, Ronald Reagan continued to admire his childhood idol's spirit and style. To Reagan, the inspirational Roosevelt remained a "soldier of freedom" who rallied dispirited Americans against the heartbreak of the Depression at home and the threat of Axis aggression abroad. Above all, he led when others faltered. Just as fascism threatened Roosevelt's America, communism, Reagan believed, had challenged global freedom since 1945.

Like millions of Americans his age, Reagan recalled with special fondness Roosevelt's use of the radio to communicate his thoughts on everything from banking reform to foreign affairs. In October 1964, when Reagan delivered his first nationally broadcast political speech, on behalf of Republican presidential candidate Barry Goldwater, he lifted verbatim one of Roosevelt's most famous lines, declaring that Americans "have a rendezvous with destiny." Reagan believed that God had selected Americans as his chosen people with a special mission.

During the 1970s, as his own ambition turned toward the White House, Reagan broadcast hundreds of short, inspirational radio talks that placed his name and ideas before a national audience. A typical commentary in May 1975 described communism as a "form of insanity" that "will one day disappear from the earth because it is contrary to human nature." Anticipating his later assertion as president that Soviet leaders would "commit any crime" to advance their cause, Reagan depicted communists as willing to carry out any crime "if it advances the cause of socialism."[2]

Once elected president, Reagan revived the lapsed practice of delivering weekly radio commentaries. In August 1984, while he engaged in banter with technicians before delivering a Saturday morning radio talk, Reagan spoke into a microphone that he did not know was activated. "My fellow Americans," he began, "I am pleased to tell you today that I've just signed legislation that will outlaw the Soviet Union forever. We begin bombing in five minutes." His making a joke of war appalled critics. Soviet officials took the off-the-cuff remark seriously enough to instruct their intelligence agents in Washington to report any signs of war preparation. The president simply laughed off criticism of his joke as if it were something his friend John Wayne might have said in a Hollywood western.

To everyone's surprise, however, less than eight years later, legislation *was* signed abolishing the Soviet Union. On Christmas day 1991, Soviet president Mikhail Gorbachev issued a decree dissolving the crumbling communist empire. With this final act, Gorbachev turned over authority to the elected leader of Russia, Boris Yeltsin. Although by then the former president's mind was clouded by the ravages of Alzheimer's disease, his many admirers and even some of his critics credited "the Great Communicator," as journalists dubbed him, with the leadership and determination that culminated in America's Cold War victory.

Reagan spoke forcefully about the division he saw between the peaceful democratic world of America and its allies and the aggressive web of communist dictatorships controlled by Moscow. As a candidate in 1980 and often thereafter, he remarked that the Soviet Union "underlies all the unrest that is going on" in the world. If "they weren't engaged in this game of dominos, there wouldn't be any hotspots in the world." Reagan also stressed his religious antipathy for communism, as in an address to the National Association of Evangelicals on March 8, 1983. The Soviet Union, he declared, was "the focus of evil in the modern world," truly an "evil empire."[3]

Reagan, his supporters stressed, recognized a simple truth that more sophisticated observers sometimes ignored: the Soviet Union was doomed to fall. In addressing the British Parliament on June 8, 1982, the president dismissed the Soviet Union as a force that "runs against the tide of history." With its economic, political, and social system all "astounding" failures, he consigned communism to the "ash heap of history." Although Reagan's perception of the Soviet Union might be "primitive," as CIA deputy director Robert Gates described it, it coincided with reality. The president's clarity of vision, his admirers believed, allowed him to see the future in ways that eluded more nuanced thinkers.[4]

While campaigning for the White House, Reagan insisted, "there are simple answers to complex questions." He told a gathering of veterans in August 1980 that under incumbent president Jimmy Carter America suffered from what he called the "Vietnam syndrome," an unwillingness to use force to resist Soviet pressure or to defend foreign friends and interests. This reluctance explained why American diplomats in 1979 had been seized and held as hostages in Iran while Soviet troops occupied Afghanistan and Moscow-backed insurgents made a play for power in Central America and Africa. Reagan traced the problem to the U.S. failure to win in Vietnam and a guilt complex left over from that war. "It's time," he told the cheering veterans, "we recognize that ours, in truth, was a noble cause." Alexander Haig, whom the newly elected Reagan named secretary of state in 1981, echoed this theme. The American people were ready to "shed their sackcloth and ashes." Taking a cue from the president's call in his inaugural address to "dream heroic dreams," the new administration moved to restore the nation's military superiority, defend allies, and, in what was later informally called the "Reagan doctrine," assist anticommunist movements throughout the world. Not by chance, the president's aides explained, did Iran release its long-held American captives just as Reagan took the presidential oath on January 20, 1981.[5]

Reagan's personal as well as his administration's approach to world affairs rested on a key assumption: since the Nixon administration, the United States had pursued a misguided policy of détente toward the Soviet Union. This effort to reduce superpower rivalry relied on arms control agreements, expanded trade, and an acceptance by each side in the Cold War of the other's legitimate security interests. At his first press conference, on January 29, 1981, Reagan echoed the complaints of conservative strategists that détente had become a "one-way street," little more than a smoke screen behind which the Soviets had expanded their strategic nuclear arsenal, cheated on arms control treaties, and supported communist insurgents in the third world. By achieving military superiority, he argued, the Soviet Union was on track to dominate the third world and isolate the United States without fear of retaliation. Reagan saw his historic mission as reversing this flow of power and delegitimizing the Soviet Union.[6]

Although he never asserted this publicly (and his aides claimed this as a strategy only after he left office), Reagan was said to believe that the inherent weakness of the communist system made the Soviet Union vulnerable to American economic pressure. By blocking access to Western technology and markets, Washington could cripple the inefficient Soviet economy. Simultaneously, rising American defense expenditures would overstress Soviet industry if it tried to match the rapid buildup. According to several high officials who spoke out after 1989, the plan to cripple the Kremlin through an arms race and economic warfare formed a centerpiece of Reagan's strategy to win the Cold War.[7]

In addition to bringing military and economic pressure to bear, Reagan, prodded by CIA director, William Casey, confronted Soviet proxies in Poland, Afghanistan, Lebanon, Angola, Mozambique, El Salvador, Grenada, and Nicaragua. By defeating the Soviets in these proxy wars, Casey argued, the United States could undermine the appeal of communism and unravel Soviet self-confidence, creating a sort of Vietnam syndrome in reverse. Ultimately, the Soviet Union would have no choice but to fundamentally alter its foreign and domestic policies. Diplomacy and negotiations with the Soviets would, at most, be an afterthought to certify American supremacy.

During his first five years in office, Reagan justified shunning talks with Moscow for two reasons. The United States, he insisted, must negotiate from strength. Even with record levels of defense spending, it would take several years to restore military superiority. Also, he quipped in response to a journalist's question, how could he meet his Soviet counterparts when "they keep dying on me." This reference to the decrepit health of Soviet leaders—and, implicitly, to his own vitality despite age—deflected public criticism. But at a more basic level, well into his second term, Reagan found himself pulled in different directions by advisers who disagreed on fundamentals and disliked each other almost as much as they hated communism.

Administration Infighting

Reagan's senior foreign policy advisers shared his general antipathy toward the Soviet Union and a determination to build up American military strength; but that was about all they agreed on. Alexander Haig, who served as Reagan's first secretary of state, described the White House "as mysterious as a ghost ship. You heard the creak of the rigging and the groan of the timbers and sometimes even glimpsed the crew on deck." But he had no idea "which of the crew was at the helm." Haig considered the president a "cipher" who virtually never discussed foreign policy with him.[8]

Many successful presidents, such as Franklin Roosevelt and Dwight Eisenhower, played off contentious aides to achieve a policy consensus. This "hidden hand" approach of allowing subordinates to take the credit —or heat—could provide valuable political cover. But Reagan's distance from policy details was of a wholly different order. Even his closest aides, like CIA director Casey, were taken aback by their boss's passivity. With few exceptions, such as missile defense and Iran-contra, Reagan initiated nothing and issued few orders. The president who came across so forcefully in scripted television speeches on the Soviet threat lost focus off camera. At meetings with his foreign policy advisers, the president frequently read from amusing letters or press clippings sent to him by admiring citizens. Then he often fell silent and exhibited what one aide called his "glassy-eyed look." If his staff reached a consensus, he endorsed it. If not, he deferred deciding. Reagan's aides kept his attention at meetings by putting on a slide or video show that presented simple, sometimes simplistic, alternatives. After initiating a policy, the president rarely followed up on it.[9]

Reagan's three closest aides during his first term, Chief of Staff James Baker, deputy chief Michael Deaver, and counselor Edwin Meese, carefully controlled the president's domestic and diplomatic agendas. The so-called troika met each morning to review the past day's events and current day's plans. One of the three men sat in with Reagan on virtually every meeting.

Baker, Deaver, and Meese wanted to prevent the emergence of a powerful national security adviser, in the mold of Henry Kissinger. Thus, the first four national security advisers, Richard Allen, William Clark, Robert McFarlane, and John Poindexter, were relatively marginal figures in the administration. Secretary of State Haig, who barely knew his boss, also remained outside Reagan's inner circle. George P. Shultz, who succeeded Haig in June 1982, ultimately emerged as the most influential and respected member of Reagan's cabinet; but his role remained muted during the first term while his two principal rivals, Defense Secretary Caspar Weinberger and CIA director William Casey, often undercut him.

Broadly speaking, pragmatists and ideologues competed for Reagan's attention. Pragmatists, including Haig, Shultz, Baker, Deaver, and Nancy Reagan, believed that as the United States adopted a stronger military posture, it should resume arms control and other negotiations with the Soviets from a position of strength. Hardliners, or so-called neoconservatives, within the administration, including Weinberger, Casey, United Nations (UN) ambassador Jeane Kirkpatrick, and Pentagon adviser Richard Perle, rejected entirely the notion of bargaining with the Soviets. Better to rearm and challenge Moscow on all fronts.

James Baker recalled that during Reagan's first six years his foreign policy structure "was often a witches' brew of intrigue" and competing agendas. Amid bureaucratic infighting, no one knew exactly what the president wanted. Reagan's fifth and sixth national security advisers, Frank Carlucci and Colin Powell, were forced to decide on their own a fundamental arms control question because they could not get the president to make a decision. As Powell recalled, a frustrated Carlucci "moaned" as they left a meeting, "My God, we didn't sign on to run this country."[10]

Economic adviser Martin Anderson, a close associate of the president, acknowledged this same trait. "We just accepted Reagan as he was," Anderson recalled, "and adjusted ourselves to his manner." Everyone "compensated for the fact that he made decisions like an ancient king or a Turkish pasha, passively letting his subjects serve him." Novelist John

Updike's account of life in the 1980s captured this quality. "Reagan," he wrote, "had that dream distance; the powerful thing about him as president was that you never knew how much he knew, nothing or everything, he was like God that way, you had to do a lot of it yourself."[11]

Defense Secretary Weinberger, an unwavering opponent of negotiations with Moscow, pushed continuously for additional military spending. At the same time, he discouraged committing American forces to regional conflicts. Taking casualties in murky causes, Weinberger worried, undermined public support for rearmament. Secretary of State Shultz, in contrast, believed that a powerful military would induce the Soviets to talk on American terms and allow Reagan to meet communist challenges in places like Central America. At one cabinet meeting an exasperated Shultz snapped at the defense secretary, "If you are not willing to use force, maybe we should cut your budget." Reagan, who found it easier to stand up to the Soviets than to his own bickering aides, declined to overrule either man. Instead, he asked his contentious advisers to settle their differences among themselves, a solution that National Security Council (NSC) head Robert McFarlane described as "intrinsically unworkable." The standoff between Shultz and Weinberger permitted CIA director Casey to win Reagan's backing for risky covert operations, at least one of which—the Iran-contra scandal—nearly sank the administration.[12]

The Military Buildup and Star Wars

In explaining his determination to boost the arms budget, Reagan declared that "defense is not a budget issue . . . you spend what you need." Surprisingly, Jimmy Carter had agreed. Defying the notion that he had cowered before the Soviets, Carter's final defense budget had proposed a 5 percent increase annually for the next five years. Reagan built on the base set out by his predecessor.[13]

Budget Director David Stockman realized that the new administration's plan for increased defense spending contained a mathematical error that would boost the military budget for the next few years by $200 billion more than Reagan had called for. When Stockman tried to correct the error, Defense Secretary Weinberger balked and took his case to the White House.

Weinberger stressed "how awesome the Soviets were and how far behind we were." Anyone cutting a nickel out of the military budget, he implied, "wanted to keep us behind the Russians." Weinberger's show-and-tell display superimposed Soviet defense plants on a map of Washington. Other illustrations depicted Soviet nuclear and conventional forces dwarfing those of the free world. "Sir, our B-52 planes are older than their pilots," the defense secretary remarked while the president nodded in agreement.

As Stockman gazed in disbelief, Weinberger displayed a cartoon depicting three soldiers. One, a pygmy carrying no weapon, represented the Carter budget. The second, a bespectacled wimp resembling Woody Allen, carried a tiny rifle. This represented Stockman's slightly reduced military budget. The final illustration, "GI Joe himself, 190 pounds of fighting man, all decked out in helmet and flak jacket, and pointing an M-60 machine gun," represented Weinberger's plan, which Reagan endorsed.[14]

During the next five years the military share of the gross national product grew from 5.7 percent to 7.4 percent. In real terms, military spending increased 50 percent, totaling $1.5 trillion. By 1985, the Pentagon spent $300 billion annually, or more than $30 million per hour. Most of this money went for new weapons like neutron bombs designed to irradiate attacking Soviet forces; a hundred MX intercontinental missiles, each capable of delivering ten nuclear warheads with pinpoint accuracy; the B-1 intercontinental bomber to replace the aging B-52; radar-avoiding stealth bombers and fighter planes; new D-5 submarine-launched missiles; intermediate range cruise and Pershing II missiles; a 600-ship navy; and antimissile research.

Many of these expensive weapons caused unintended problems. No one, including Reagan's congressional supporters, wanted MX missiles based in their state, since the missiles tempted the Soviets to launch a first strike. Ultimately, the missiles were housed in existing silos that Reagan had previously criticized as vulnerable to Soviet attack. The B-1 bomber had so many technical problems that it remained grounded most of the time and never replaced the B-52. In fact, the B-52 remained the military workhorse of the U.S. Air Force well into the twenty-first century, outlasting many of the new aircraft designed to replace it. Stealth technology proved difficult to perfect until the 1990s and planes that utilized it were notoriously hard to maintain. Billions were spent on antimissile research but no system emerged.

Although Reagan had denounced previous arms control agreements with the Soviets as "fatally flawed," he did not abrogate them. In 1982 and 1983, the Joint Chiefs cautioned Reagan that the unratified Strategic Arms

Limitations Treaty (SALT) II negotiated by President Carter actually *enhanced* U.S. security—even if the Kremlin cheated at the margins—by placing caps on the number of Soviet strategic weapons. Reagan continued to denounce SALT II, but generally adhered to the pact.

One of Reagan's most cherished military innovations—the Strategic Defense Initiative (SDI)—represented an effort to beat the Soviets technologically and, perhaps, bankrupt them. Despite much criticism of the scheme in the 1980s and beyond, Reagan's defenders, like British prime minister Thatcher, argued that the president's "original decision" to support missile defense "was the single most important of his presidency."[15]

Shortly before he took office, Reagan reportedly expressed shock at learning that in a nuclear war more than half of all Americans would quickly perish. The president partly blamed the policy of mutual assured destruction (MAD), comparing it to two rivals (say, the United States and the USSR) pointing loaded guns at each other and hoping that neither would pull the trigger. In fact, MAD presumed that neither gunman would fire since to do so would bring certain retaliation from surviving weapons, no matter who shot first.

Initially, the Reagan administration tried to dampen fears of nuclear holocaust by claiming that a revived fallout shelter program could save millions of lives. But when Pentagon spokesman T.K. Jones announced that most Americans could survive nuclear war if only they took time to "dig a hole, cover it with a couple of doors, and then throw some dirt on top," the campaign became an object of derision.[16]

Although most Americans supported Reagan's overall tough stand, during 1982 and 1983, as many as 70 percent of Americans, along with a growing number of clergy and members of Congress, questioned Reagan's nuclear arms buildup. Many voiced approval of a nuclear freeze movement that called for capping weapons at current levels. A best-selling book by Jonathan Schell, *The Fate of the Earth* (1982), depicted in gruesome detail the effect of a single hydrogen bomb dropped on New York City. On October 26, 1982, the *New York Times* reported that the nation's Roman Catholic bishops issued a pastoral letter that decried nuclear weapons as "immoral" and the arms race as "robbery of the poor." These misgivings troubled the president, who, despite his rhetoric, harbored doubts about the morality of nuclear weapons.

In the late 1970s, physicist Dr. Edward Teller and retired air force general Daniel Graham, who headed a group called High Frontier, told Reagan of the possibility of an antimissile shield. At an Oval Office meeting early in 1983, Teller described progress (bogus, it turned out) in building a nuclear-powered X-ray laser that if based in space could generate energy beams to shoot down Soviet missiles shortly after their launch. This space shield concept may have rekindled Reagan's memories of a 1940 movie *Murder in the Air,* in which he, playing secret agent Brass Bancroft, protects an "inertia projector" that could stop enemy aircraft in flight.[17]

The president latched on to the concept of a space shield and made it one of his most intense personal causes. Nuclear war, he told friends, might be Armageddon, the biblically prophesied battle before Christ's return. Perhaps SDI could prevent it. Just how a technological fix would prevent a rain of ruin ordained by God was unclear. But SDI promised a range of material as well as spiritual rewards.

The Joint Chiefs of Staff doubted the practicability of a leakproof umbrella, but thought it might be possible to devise a system to protect a small number of American nuclear missile sites—not civilians—from a Soviet attack. This would enhance, not replace, deterrence, as Reagan erroneously believed. Defense contractors and university scientists relished the prospect of massive research and development contracts that would flow from such a program. Some arms control experts hoped to use the leverage of an antimissile system to prod the Soviets into a new round of strategic arms control negotiations on American terms. Administration hard-liners who opposed any dealings with Moscow hoped that SDI would outrage the Soviets and open the way for an even larger arms buildup by the United States.

Virtually alone, Reagan clung to the belief that he was talking about a leakproof shield capable of protecting American civilians, missiles, and allies. With this belief in mind, he latched on to a statement by Army Chief of Staff General John W. Vesey that it would be "better to protect the American people than to avenge them." On March 23, 1983, Reagan shared what he called his "vision" with the American people, in a televised address that spoke of rendering Soviet missiles "impotent and obsolete" by destroying them before they "reached our own soil or that of our allies." In an adroit maneuver, SDI chronicler Frances Fitzgerald noted, Reagan had "appropriated the language of the anti-nuclear movement" even as he endorsed a plan to expand the nuclear arms race to outer space.[18] Like Prime Minister Thatcher, some of Reagan's advisers later described Reagan's fixation on SDI—or Star Wars, as his critics promptly dubbed it—as a brilliant deception. Deputy CIA director Gates argued that SDI did not even need to work, since the mere concept stoked terror inside the Kremlin. SDI represented the triple threat of superior American technology, managerial skills, and wealth harnessed to a project that the Soviets could not possibly hope to match. In fact, Gates argued, the only real believers in SDI were Reagan and the Soviet Politburo. Gates and Thatcher imply that Reagan intuitively sensed that SDI was a "symbolic threat" to the Soviets, a sort of "perfect storm" that would cripple Moscow.[19]

Gates justified SDI in part because the Soviets themselves invested heavily in antimissile research. Of course, he admitted, they lacked the requisite technology to achieve much of value. At the same time, Gates interpreted Soviet opposition to SDI as proof of their frustration over the prospect of having spent billions of rubles on a nuclear arsenal that might become obsolete.

Even Gates recognized that Soviet hostility toward SDI stemmed from several sources. Aside from Reagan, virtually no one believed that the United States could in the near future deploy an antimissile system capable of neutralizing a full Soviet attack. The Pentagon itself estimated that it might require several thousand flights of America's fickle space shuttle to boost all SDI components into orbit. Since the shuttle flew only a few times each year, at this pace deployment of the system might take a century! In theory, the United States *might* more rapidly develop a "leaky" system capable of shooting down a small number of enemy rockets. From the Soviet perspective, this could enable the United States to launch a first strike and sit back with enough antimissile capacity to withstand weak Soviet retaliation—neutralizing MAD.

Some who served Reagan later argued that SDI was part of the "bankrupt the Soviets" strategy hatched in 1981–1982; but other Reagan advisers closely involved with SDI dispute this account. CIA deputy director Robert Gates found little evidence to suggest that Soviet efforts to counter SDI overstressed the Soviet economy. Arms control negotiator Lieutenant General Edward L. Rowny doubted that scholars would discover in the archival record "any serious talk about [spending the Soviets into the ground] at all." Rowny, along with national security adviser Robert McFarlane, argued that Reagan pushed the plan primarily because he believed it would counter Soviet missile strength and secondarily because he thought it might actually save the United States money in its ongoing arms competition with the Soviets.[20]

Although Reagan offered little beyond generalities in defense of

SDI, his talk of abandoning the concept of mutual assured destruction and pulling out of the 1972 antiballistic missile treaty (ABM) aroused grave anxiety in Moscow. As discussed below, it may have delayed, rather than accelerated, Soviet-American cooperation. Under Reagan, the United States spent nearly $20 billion on antimissile research. After 1989, presidents George H.W. Bush, Bill Clinton, and George W. Bush spent about $60 billion more on aspects of this project. In 2001, President George W. Bush put antimissile defense back on the fast track. In 2004 the United States began to deploy a largely untested missile defense system in Alaska designed to intercept a handful of rockets that might be launched by North Korea or another "rogue state." This ground-based program was not directly related to Reagan's concept of SDI. Despite the lack of hard evidence, conservatives argue that Reagan's dream—or bluff—helped break the Cold War stalemate and offered greater protection to America.

The Economic Cold War

In addition to bulking up American military strength, Reagan believed the United States should do more to undermine the Soviet economy. In March 1982, he received a briefing that years later he said convinced him that the Soviets were "in very bad shape and if we can cut off their credit they'll have to yell 'uncle' or starve." CIA director Casey assured the president that the agency could identify Soviet vulnerabilities and produce a guide for economic warfare. Assuring Reagan that "we can do them in," Casey provided "vulnerability assessments" that became part of the president's regular reading.[21]

Reagan had long considered the Soviet system inherently unstable. In a May 1975 radio commentary, for example, he declared "communism is neither an economic or a political system—it is a form of insanity." In radio remarks of September 1979, he endorsed the notion that "given our industrial superiority," America "could not possibly lose . . . an unrestrained arms race."[22]

Although Reagan and his aides shared a general belief in a weak and vulnerable Soviet economy, they disagreed on what, if anything, they should do about it. National security adviser Robert McFarlane recalled that "many in Reagan's own cabinet . . . didn't agree with him" that "a more energetic competition could impose such burdens as to bring down the Soviet Union." Douglas MacEachin, director of the CIA's Office of

Soviet Analysis from 1984 to 1989, voiced similar doubts. America's Soviet experts were "virtually unanimous" that the communist system had reached a "near critical" mass of social and economic problems. But the same matrix of rigid central controls that caused these problems made it likely that the Soviet Union would continue to muddle along in slow decline, perhaps for decades. To be sure, some of Reagan's policies "imposed costs" on Moscow, but, McFarlane concluded, "80 to 90 percent of what happened to the USSR was because Marxism was a dumb idea."[23]

After the Soviet collapse, strident ideologues like Richard Perle, and scholar and NSC staff member Richard Pipes took credit for implementing an economic warfare strategy. But the two advisers who ultimately influenced Reagan's most important Soviet initiatives from 1983 onward, career diplomat Jack Matlock and Secretary of State George Shultz, dispute claims that Reagan pursed a master plan to "bring down" the evil empire. "None of the key players," Matlock remarked in 1998, "were operating from the assumption that we were going to bring them down. . . . That's all thinking after the fact." The goal was always "to give the Soviets incentives to bring the Cold War to an end." Shultz argued this point forcefully to Reagan in a 1983 report that predicted a long period of ongoing competition in Soviet-American relations. Shultz hoped that a restored dialogue with the Soviets, in place of name-calling, might lead to "actual improvement" in how the two powers got along. The Soviet system had "serious weaknesses," Shultz affirmed, "but it would be a mistake to assume that the Soviet capacity for competition with us will diminish at any time during your presidency."[24]

Foreign experts had great difficulty assessing the Soviet economy. It had recovered from the devastation of World War II to become, despite chronic agricultural shortages, one of the world's biggest producers of steel, cement, fertilizer, tractors, and machine tools. To achieve these levels of production in what everyone recognized were inefficient factories, Soviet industry utilized—and often squandered—the nation's vast natural resource base. To cover the costs of vital imports and food, the Soviets exported large amounts of oil and precious metals.

Severe problems lurked beneath the facade of success. The industrial growth rate began to decline after 1980. The quality of Soviet life, as measured by rates of infant mortality, longevity, alcoholism, and so on, was deteriorating. The technology divide between the Western economies and Japan on the one hand and the Soviet bloc on the other hand had become a yawning chasm by the time Reagan became president. Market economies utilized computers, high technology, and information management to surge ahead. The Soviet command system mobilized labor and resources, but not creativity or innovation. Fearful of losing control, Soviet managers frowned on basic tools like personal computers and photocopiers. As one Kremlin leader observed privately in the early 1980s, "the Soviet economy is not in much better shape than that of Poland."[25]

After 1981, Reagan moved to deny the Soviets easy access to Western technology and credit. The United States pressed its European and Japanese allies to cancel or restrict sales of oil and gas drilling and pipeline technology to the Soviet Union. A secret U.S. initiative provided flawed computer programs to the Soviets that contributed to a massive pipeline explosion. CIA director Casey and Defense Secretary Weinberger promoted arms sales to Saudi Arabia as a way of convincing the Arab state to expand oil pumping. Increased Saudi production not only lowered prices to U.S. consumers, but also reduced revenues the Soviets earned from petroleum exports. By 1985, partly in response to American policy, the Saudis raised production from 2 million barrels per day to almost 9 million. This increase drove down prices from about $30 per barrel to less than half that amount, depriving the Soviets of billions of dollars in export sales.[26]

Several Reagan aides attributed the collapse of the Soviet Union to this economic warfare strategy. However, the facts suggest otherwise. As early as 1984, barely three years after imposing sanctions, a year and a half before reformer Mikhail Gorbachev assumed power, and seven years before the Soviet collapse, Reagan actually began lifting many of the sanctions. The president acted when it became clear that the sanctions had many unintended consequences. For example, pressure on U.S. allies to stop selling gas and oil drilling and pipeline technology to Moscow infuriated the British, French, Germans, and Japanese, who, unlike the Americans, wanted to import more Soviet energy supplies. In response to their complaints, Reagan relaxed many trade restrictions.

The fact that the United States insisted on its own right to sell the Soviets what it wanted angered the Europeans and Japanese. In 1980, President Carter had retaliated against the Soviet invasion of Afghanistan by placing an embargo on U.S. grain sales to Moscow, even though this annoyed midwestern farmers and hurt his own reelection prospects. Despite Reagan's rhetorical tough line and effort to choke off foreign trade with the Soviets, soon after taking office he *resumed* grain sales to the

Soviet Union, largely to appease farmers. Foreign observers considered this grossly hypocritical.

Claims by Reagan's advisers that they engineered the Saudi decision in 1985 to turn on the oil spigot and quadruple production proved more complicated than they first appeared. Driving the price of petroleum down by more than 50 percent dried up much of the foreign currency earned by Soviet oil exports, but at an especially great cost to the U.S. energy sector. Falling prices devastated many small and medium producers in the "oil patch" states of the American West. By the late 1980s, tumbling property values in the region sped the collapse of the shaky savings and loan (S&L) industry. The scope of the banking crisis did not become apparent until after Reagan left office. The federal bailout of bankrupt S&Ls in the early 1990s cost American taxpayers several hundred billion dollars.[27]

Reagan's foreign policy had other unintended economic results. To finance the huge military buildup while also cutting taxes and to prevent the already record budget deficit from growing larger, the Reagan Treasury Department borrowed massively from foreign investors and governments. Reagan inherited a cumulative national debt of just under $1 trillion in 1981. Over the next eight years, annual budget shortfalls ranged from $128 billion to over $200 billion. By 1989, federal indebtedness had tripled, to a record $2.7 trillion.

Increasingly, Japanese, Saudi, German, and other foreign sources purchased the U.S. Treasury notes and bonds that financed the deficit resulting from defense increases and tax shortfalls. By the end of Reagan's presidency, foreign creditors held nearly 20 percent of the national debt, a historic high. Under Reagan, the nation's foreign trade imbalance also grew dramatically. The cumulative foreign trade deficit of the United States totaled nearly $1 trillion by 1989.

During the 1980s, the United States changed from the world's biggest creditor nation to the largest debtor. A growing portion of the interest paid on debt and of profits earned from consumer purchases flowed into the hands of foreign investors. But when a reporter asked Reagan what he thought of this seismic change, he simply denied it was so.[28]

Terrorism, Democracy, and Covert Warfare

Reagan and leading members of his administration portrayed terrorism in the Middle East and against American interests elsewhere as among the gravest threats confronting the United States. In speeches delivered within days of taking office, the president and his new secretary of state issued clear warnings. "Let terrorists beware," Reagan declared, "our policy will be one of swift and effective retribution." In 1985 he repeated "America will never make concessions to terrorists" and condemned Iran and Libya as examples of "outlaw states . . . run by the strangest collection of misfits, Looney Tunes and squalid criminals since the advent of the Third Reich."

In a backhanded slap at President Carter, the Reagan administration abandoned the policy of putting pressure on pro-American dictatorships to improve their human rights performance. The president praised the ideas of Jeane Kirkpatrick (whom he named as ambassador to the United Nations), voiced in an article she wrote for the conservative journal *Commentary* in 1979. Kirkpatrick berated Carter's failure to support friendly "right-wing autocracies" like those of the shah of Iran or the Samoza family of Nicaragua. Unlike left-wing regimes, she opined, pro-American dictatorships "sometimes evolve into democracies." Haig declared that the struggle against "international terrorism will take the place of human rights in our concern because it is the ultimate abuse of human rights." Reagan's strong personal attachment to anticommunist despots like Ferdinand Marcos in the Philippines and Jean Claude ("Baby Doc") Duvalier in Haiti reflected these priorities.[29]

While Reagan and Haig blamed the Soviets for terrorism in general, CIA director Casey and his deputy, Robert Gates, tried to prove that Soviet agents masterminded the 1981 attempt by a Turk to assassinate Polish-born pope John Paul II. They cited claims by journalist Claire Sterling that the gunman had worked for Soviet-controlled Bulgarian intelligence. When career State Department and CIA analysts noted that Sterling mostly recycled disinformation fed to her by U.S. intelligence agents who hoped to discredit the Soviets, Casey would not relent. Over the next four years he and Gates doggedly pursued evidence of Soviet complicity. Casey's critics guessed that his real goal was to convince Reagan to reject any dealings with a regime that tried to kill the pope.[30]

Despite efforts by Haig, Casey, and Reagan to define all terrorism as madness or a Soviet plot, the administration often bent its own rules barring support for or negotiations with groups linked to terror. Over the course of eight years, Reagan and his aides sold weapons to two nations they publicly condemned as terrorist states (Iraq and Iran), provided weapons to anticommunist guerrillas linked to terrorism in Lebanon,

Afghanistan, Africa, and Central America, and several times negotiated secretly for the release of American hostages seized by terrorists. Even some of Reagan's defenders agreed "it would be hard to imagine a case where there is a larger gap between words and action in Administration policy."[31]

Terrorism was as often a symptom as a source of regional violence. Some have described it as the atomic bomb of the weak. Grisly journalistic accounts fueled public anxiety over terrorism. The kidnapping of a handful of Americans in Lebanon, occasional aircraft and ship hijackings, and the bombing of several airliners were despicable but marginal acts in the world arena. In aggregate during the 1980s, about as many American civilians were killed by lightning while playing golf as died at the hands of terrorists. Terrorism became a popular obsession partly because of media hype and partly because President Reagan made it so. Until September 11, 2001, the two deadliest foreign terrorist attacks against Americans occurred during the Reagan administration. In two bombings in Lebanon during 1983, nearly 300 marines and embassy personnel died. The December 1988 bombing of a Pan Am flight over Scotland killed 259 on board and 11 people on the ground.

Although conservatives dismissed Jimmy Carter as a wimp, during 1979 and 1980 his administration initiated both a major arms buildup (that set the stage for many of the weapons systems attributed to Reagan) and several of the covert operations credited to his successor. Even if many Americans doubted his resolve, the Soviets, CIA deputy director Gates asserted, "saw Carter as a committed ideological foe as well as a geopolitical adversary." Carter "prepared the ground work for Reagan in the strategic arena, in confronting the Soviets" in the third world.[32]

CIA Director Casey, with help from the National Security Council, served as the administration's coordinator of policies on terrorism and covert challenges to the Soviet Union. Casey (a veteran of the World War II–era Office of Strategic Services and a wealthy Wall Street investor who managed Reagan's 1980 election campaign), his deputy recalled, "truly admired Reagan." But in private even he "would complain about the President's lack of interest in specifics, his unwillingness to take hard decisions . . . and his rather simplistic view of the world." Reagan's inner circle, Baker, Meese, and especially Deaver, worried that the spy chief "played to Reagan's dark side." Casey's habit of mumbling, combined with the president's impaired hearing, often left Reagan's aides unsure what the two men discussed or agreed upon. After Reagan–Casey meetings, Deaver debriefed his boss. If Casey had sold the president on some wild scheme, Deaver passed word to Baker, who spoke with Nancy Reagan and arranged for the first lady to talk her husband out of it.[33]

Casey favored arming anticommunist groups around the world because of his belief that the Soviet Union was "tremendously overextended and vulnerable." If America challenged the Soviets everywhere and defeated them even in one place, "that will shatter the mythology . . . and it will all start to unravel." Reagan endorsed this concept, sometimes called the Reagan doctrine, in several internal policy papers and in a widely cited speech delivered at his alma mater, Eureka College in Illinois, on May 9, 1982, where he promised active support for people fighting communism, wherever they were.[34]

Reagan inherited an unstable, violent Middle East and left the region in pretty much the same condition. Conflicts between the Israelis and Palestinians, among Lebanese factions, within Afghanistan, and between Iraq and Iran continued during the 1980s and set the stage for future problems, some involving terrorism aimed directly at the United States.

In the early 1980s, Lebanese religious and political factions resumed their periodic civil slaughter, with Israel and Syria backing armed groups. When the White House criticized Secretary of State Haig's June 1982 support for an Israeli invasion of Lebanon, he quit abruptly. George Shultz, named as Haig's successor, had no more success in stabilizing the area.

As chaos engulfed Lebanon, the United States dispatched marines to join French and Italian troops as peacekeepers. At times, the marines assisted Christian militias fighting Muslim forces backed by Syria. In response, on April 18, 1983, a suicide squad blew up the U.S. embassy in Beirut, killing sixty-three people. U.S. Navy ships off Lebanon then bombarded several Islamic strongholds. On October 23, a Muslim suicide bomber retaliated by driving a truck filled with explosives into a U.S. Marine barracks near the Beirut airport, killing 241 Americans.

President Reagan offered a stirring tribute to the fallen marines, but no credible explanation of their mission or the reason for their deaths. A few months later, in his 1984 State of the Union address, he described the marine presence as "central to our credibility on a global scale." Two weeks later, without explanation, he withdrew American forces from Beirut.

Public reaction to the disaster was muted, in part because of lavish media attention focused on Grenada, a tiny Caribbean island. Although

Marxists had ruled Grenada since 1979, neither the Carter nor Reagan administrations had paid much attention to it. The only American presence on the island consisted of 500 students enrolled in a private medical college. A contingent of armed Cuban construction workers labored on an airport designed to boost tourism (as Grenada claimed) or to serve as a Soviet-Cuban air base (as Washington asserted).

A more militant Marxist faction seized control of Grenada on October 12, 1983. Immediately after the catastrophe in Beirut on October 23, Reagan declared that the American students on Grenada might become hostages, although none had been threatened. On October 25, he ordered thousands of marines and amphibious army troops to liberate Grenada and the American students from what he called a "brutal gang of thugs."[35]

In an action that was more of a comic opera than a war, the U.S. invaders quickly secured the island. The students were flown home and a photograph of one kissing American soil became a staple in the president's reelection commercials. As if to compensate for the Beirut debacle, the Pentagon awarded an unprecedented 8,000 medals to members of the assault force. Free elections restored representative government to the island. Most Americans approved the operation, telling pollsters in effect they were pleased that the United States had won one for a change. Ironically, news coverage of the invasion alerted many Americans to Grenada's lovely beaches and eventually sparked a tourist boom, facilitated by the Cuban-built airport!

Washington focused much of its antiterrorist sentiment during the 1980s on Libya's demagogic and oil-rich strongman, Muammar Qaddafi. Flush with cash, he purchased Soviet weapons and funded several terrorist groups in the region. To contain the threat, the U.S. Navy deployed ships close to Libya and engaged Qaddafi's air force in several dogfights. In April 1986, after Libyan agents were linked to the bombing of a Berlin nightclub frequented by American GIs, Reagan condemned Qaddafi as the "mad dog of the Middle East."[36] He ordered American planes to bomb targets in Tripoli, including Qaddafi's residence where his infant daughter was killed.

Following the attack, Libya and the United States engaged most in verbal warfare. Reagan, his aides quipped, had put Qaddafi "back in his box."[37] In fact, plummeting oil prices and feuds between Libya and its North African neighbors constrained Qaddafi as much as anything. Two years later, however, in December 1988, Libyan agents planted a bomb aboard a Pan Am jet that exploded over Scotland, killing 270 people.[38]

The most intense violence in the Middle East occurred during a nine-year war between Iraq and Iran that started in 1980. Fought over regional influence, oil, and deepwater ports, the war claimed nearly 2 million lives before fighting ceased in 1988. The war put the United States in an awkward position. Understandably, Washington opposed both the zealous expansion efforts by Iran's Islamist fundamentalist rulers and the drive by the secular but thuggish Iraqi ruler, Saddam Hussein, to dominate the Persian Gulf and Arabian Peninsula. A lopsided victory by either side might further destabilize the oil-rich region. To prevent this outcome, Reagan authorized covert military assistance to both nations. Aid flowed to both sides depending on the battlefield situation. To bolster Iraqi dictator Saddam Hussein, the Reagan administration muted criticism of his regime even when he used poison gas to kill tens of thousands of dissident Kurds (an ethnic minority living in northern Iraq) and invading Iranian soldiers. In December 1983, Reagan sent a top Pentagon aide, Donald Rumsfeld (later secretary of defense), on a goodwill mission to Baghdad designed to boost U.S.-Iraqi trade and cooperation. In 1988, war-weary Iran and Iraq agreed to a cease-fire—with both sides nursing deep resentment against the United States.

Among the several Reagan-era interventions, Afghanistan is often praised as the most successful. In 1979, the Soviets invaded that bleak land on their southern border in an effort to shore up a shaky native communist regime established a few years earlier. Soon, over 100,000 Soviet soldiers became trapped in a vicious guerrilla war against mujahideen, or freedom fighters, many of whom were inspired by fundamentalist Islam.

President Carter, encouraged by his national security adviser, Zbigniew Brzezinski who spoke of trapping the Soviets in something like their own Vietnam, had initiated aid to these anti-Soviet guerrillas. The Reagan administration greatly expanded assistance. In 1982, CIA director William Casey, among other Americans, fell under the sway of Pakistani strongman Mohammed Zia ul-Haq. Zia convinced his American friends that the Soviets viewed Afghanistan as a platform for wider expansion. Moscow, he argued, had revived a nineteenth-century czarist strategy ("The Great Game") aimed at dominating the Persian Gulf, Pakistan, and India. Casey's idea of building up the mujahideen into a serious fighting force found favor with a flamboyant Texas congressman, Charlie Wilson, who persuaded his colleagues to fund a major military aid program. By 1986, the Afghan guerrillas received U.S. antiaircraft missiles and other advanced weaponry that took a heavy toll on Soviet forces.[39]

To deliver American weapons, the Reagan administration worked closely with Afghanistan's neighbors, China and Pakistan. Chinese communist leaders resented the Soviets almost as much as did the anticommunist Reagan. Their cooperation convinced the president, a longtime supporter of Taiwan, to mute his past criticism of the People's Republic. Pakistan drove a harder bargain. Zia insisted that Washington provide his repressive regime with substantial military, economic, and political support. With tacit U.S. approval, Pakistan began developing its own nuclear arsenal and allowed a group of scientists and military officers to sell nuclear technology to other nations, including Libya and North Korea. Pakistan also evolved into a training camp for Islamist fundamentalists from throughout the world who were drawn to the fight in nearby Afghanistan. Among those arriving was Osama bin Laden, a wealthy Saudi who viewed the anti-Soviet struggle as the first phase in a wider war against Western infidels. At the time, the Reagan administration asked few questions about the beliefs or ultimate goals of its allies so long as they took an anti-Soviet stance.

From 1981 to 1986, Reagan authorized several other CIA covert operations. The agency provided money to sustain the Solidarity labor movement challenging communist domination of Poland and gave weapons to anti-Vietnamese guerrillas in Cambodia. The CIA also supported guerrilla armies in Angola and Mozambique that were battling Soviet and Cuban-backed movements. Although aid to Solidarity—like the Afghan resistance—enjoyed broad support among Americans and Europeans, the operations in Cambodia and Africa allied the United States with brutal, antidemocratic groups.

In spite of claims that these operations achieved positive results, the record is, at best, mixed. The only real "victories" in these shadow wars came in Poland, where American financial (not military) support went to genuine democrats with popular backing, and in Afghanistan, where weapons helped the dedicated but undemocratic guerrillas stymie the Soviets. CIA-backed operations in Lebanon, Southeast Asia, and Africa failed by almost any measure. Reagan's most controversial intervention took place in Central America, where his secret aid to anticommunist forces nearly ended his presidency.

From Banana Wars to Iran-Contra

President Reagan and his closest aides appeared obsessed by a perceived Soviet and Cuban threat to the Western Hemisphere. To counter this, and to erase the humiliating memory of Vietnam, the president revived the tradition of U.S. muscle flexing in Latin America. Administration rhetoric often sounded like a replay of the early Cold War. State Department and CIA spokesmen described a "Moscow-Havana" axis whose Soviet-armed Cuban agents conspired to spread revolution in both Africa and Latin America. UN ambassador Jeane Kirkpatrick called Central America and the Caribbean "the most important place in the world for us." Reagan warned that Moscow and Havana conspired to set up puppet Latin American regimes to sever the U.S. "lifeline to the outside world."

As a candidate, Reagan criticized Carter for abandoning Nicaraguan dictator Anastasio Somoza, whose family had ruled the country as a fiefdom since the 1920s. Once elected, Reagan claimed that the leftist Sandinista movement that had toppled Somoza had turned Nicaragua into a Soviet outpost and a "safe house and command post for international terror."[40] In one especially vivid presidential speech, he conjured up a vision of Sandinistas driving a convoy of armed pickup trucks north into Harlingen, Texas, a town on the Mexican border. Political satirist Garry Trudeau parodied this warning in his *Doonesbury* comic strip, depicting a group of "good ol' boys" from Harlingen peering through the sights of their hunting rifles ready to repulse an invasion.[41]

Democratic critics, like Connecticut senator Christopher Dodd, countered that Reagan and his advisers knew "as much about Central America" in the 1980s "as we knew about Indochina in 1963."[42] As a former Peace Corps volunteer in Latin America, Dodd insisted that if the region "were not racked with poverty, there would be no revolution." To counter such criticism, Reagan asked Henry Kissinger to assess the situation. In 1984 a commission led by the former secretary of state acknowledged that Soviet meddling did not cause all of Central America's problems. Still, in order to block Moscow's attempt to exploit Latin American instability, Kissinger urged increased military aid to anticommunist regimes like El Salvador and to guerrillas fighting in Nicaragua.

In spite of Reagan's passionate calls for greater U.S. involvement, the public proved apathetic when it came to Latin America. Pollsters found that most Americans did not care who dominated, say, Tegucigalpa or Managua. At the same time, however, they deferred to Reagan's judgment as long as American troops were not killed in combat. As a result, the administration focused on supplying military aid to friendly governments in the region and supporting covert warfare that placed few American lives at risk.

During the 1980s, Reagan authorized spending nearly $5 billion to shore up the government of tiny El Salvador, a nominal democracy dominated by hard-line militarists who had been battling a left-wing rebellion since 1979. A terribly poor nation in which 2 percent of the population owned nearly everything, El Salvador had been wracked by rural rebellions for most of the twentieth century. In spite of massive military aid, the Salvadoran army could not defeat the leftist rebels and their civilian allies. The army squandered much of the money while government troops and paramilitary death squads, some trained by Americans, killed about 70,000 peasants, teachers, union organizers, and church workers during the 1980s. Congress imposed a cap of a few hundred on the number of U.S. military advisers in El Salvador, but otherwise asked few questions. The brutal civil war continued until 1992, when a truce restored a semblance of representative government.[43]

The moral morass of El Salvador seemed crystal clear compared to the hole Reagan dug for himself in neighboring Nicaragua. Nothing the president did in eight years so tarnished his reputation or called into question his judgment so seriously as his decision to sell weapons to Iran as part of a scheme to ransom U.S. hostages in Beirut and fund anticommunist fighters in Central America.

Reagan accurately described Nicaragua's Sandinista leaders as dedicated Marxists who disliked the United States and received aid from Cuba and the Soviet Union. Also, as he charged, they harassed political opponents and blocked promised free elections. But Sandinista abuses paled in comparison to the violence inflicted on civilians and especially indigenous Indians by the pro-U.S. regimes of nearby El Salvador, Guatemala, and Honduras. In any case, Nicaragua was a tiny nation with fewer inhabitants than many American cities. To portray it as a real or potential threat to hemispheric security distorted reality.

Nevertheless, both Reagan and CIA director Casey saw global stakes at play. Casey, according to his deputy, Robert Gates, "became obsessed with Central America" and believed that if the United States could defeat a Soviet proxy in just one place, the entire evil empire would "unravel." "Nick-a-wog-wha," as he pronounced it, "is that place."

In 1981 Reagan ordered Casey to organize an anti-Sandinista force called the *contrarrevolucionarios,* or contras. The president praised them as "freedom fighters" and "the moral equal of our Founding Fathers." With generous U.S. aid, contra ranks swelled to between 10,000 and

20,000 men. Most of the movement's leaders were veterans of the old Samoza dictatorship, not incipient Thomas Jeffersons.[44]

When Congress questioned CIA funding of the guerrillas, Casey falsely assured the lawmakers that the contras did not intend to overthrow the Sandinistas, a regime technically at peace with the United States. Rather, U.S. aid enabled the guerrillas to interdict Sandinista military aid to Salvadoran rebels. In fact, in December 1981 Reagan had signed a secret order authorizing contra aid for the purpose of deposing the Sandinistas. In 1982, as reports surfaced linking contra attacks to thousands of civilian deaths in Nicaragua, Congress passed a resolution named for Representative Edward P. Boland that capped CIA assistance to the rebels at $24 million and ordered that none of the funds be used to topple the Nicaraguan government. In October 1984, after learning that the CIA and the contras had illegally mined Nicaraguan harbors, Congress passed a stricter version of the Boland law that barred *any* U.S. government funds going to the contras for *any* purpose.

These restrictions infuriated Reagan, who disparaged Congress as a committee of busybodies. He informed national security adviser Robert McFarlane and his deputy, Admiral John Poindexter, as well as NSC staffer Lieutenant Colonel Oliver North, "to do whatever you have to do to help these people [the contras] keep body and soul together." For a president who seldom issued clear instructions to subordinates, this was a definitive order.[45]

After conferring with Casey and several State Department officials, McFarlane, Poindexter, and North devised a scheme to "privatize" contra aid by soliciting funds from friendly foreign governments and wealthy American conservatives. North opened Swiss bank accounts into which he deposited money donated by Israel, Saudi Arabia, South Africa, South Korea, Taiwan, and Brunei, as well as oilman Nelson Bunker Hunt and beer baron Joseph Coors. Some of the foreign funds actually originated as U.S. assistance to the countries that "donated" them to the contras. Reagan also permitted his aides to deal with Panamanian strongman Manuel Noriega. Although Noriega had turned Panama into a banking and transportation haven for Colombian cocaine dealers, U.S. officials looked the other way since he allowed the CIA to use Panama as a conduit for aid to the contras. Reagan did not know—or want to know—all the details of contra aid, but McFarlane and his successor as national security adviser, John Poindexter, kept him closely informed of their activities and received his blessing.[46]

Although some two dozen senior CIA, State Department, and White House officials were linked to the illegal scheme to aid the contras, Secretary of State Shultz considered the operation foolhardy. In June 1984 he warned Reagan that soliciting funds to circumvent Congress might constitute an impeachable offense. The president understood Shultz's concern, since he quipped to aides that if the story of his assisting the contras ever got out "we'll all be hanging by our thumbs in front of the White House."[47]

In March 1986, even while Soviet-American relations were beginning to improve, Reagan delivered a dramatic televised speech warning that the Soviets and Cubans had turned Nicaragua into a base to sever U.S. access to South America, the Panama Canal, and the Caribbean sea-lanes. Moscow and Havana, he declared, had implemented the "old Communist slogan" that "the road to victory [over the United States] goes through Mexico." Congress, still awed by Reagan's popularity, bowed to his urgent plea to resume limited aid to the contras. By then, however, Reagan had approved yet another illegal scheme.[48]

Unbeknown to Congress or the public, during the previous year the illicit contra aid program had merged with ongoing, secret, and illegal contacts with Iran. Reagan had several times publicly condemned the Iranian regime as an "outlaw state" linked to terrorism. U.S. law barred selling or giving Iran any military equipment unless the president informed Congress in writing of a compelling reason to do so. Reagan found a reason, but declined to notify anyone.

For some time Reagan had been moved by the plight of seven Americans who had been kidnapped in Beirut and held as hostages by Islamist militias linked to Iran. With the exception of one hostage, CIA agent William Buckley (who was killed shortly after his abduction), all were private U.S. citizens who had remained in Lebanon despite official warnings to leave. Recalling public disgust with Carter's handling of the Iranian hostages in 1979–1980, Reagan acted boldly. In mid-1985, an Iranian businessman contacted NSC adviser Robert McFarlane and claimed that he could secure the hostages' release in return for U.S. arms sales to "moderate" elements in Iran who might take power following the death of Ayatollah Khomeini.

Despite his pledge "never to negotiate with terrorists," Reagan told McFarlane, "Gee, that sounds pretty good." In his diary, the president stressed that he liked the idea of a deal to get "our seven kidnap victims back." Building a new relationship with Iran appeared as an afterthought.

Over the next year, Reagan authorized several additional secret arms sales to Iran. Three hostages were eventually released, but three more were taken as replacements. Reagan had not only deceived Congress and broken his pledge not to bargain with terrorists, but he had created a lucrative market for seizing Americans.

This scheme took an even more bizarre turn when NSC staffer Oliver North conceived what he called a "neat idea." Why not overcharge the Iranians for the American weapons they received and use the excess profits from the sales to support the Nicaraguan contras? As North joked, the Iranians would unknowingly make a "contra-bution." Like other elements of the plan, this too violated federal law, since profits from any sale of U.S. government property, including weapons, had to be returned to the Treasury, not given to the President's pet guerrilla charity in defiance of Congress.[49]

The tangled scheme began to unravel in October 1986 when Sandinista gunners shot down a CIA-chartered plane carrying weapons to the contras. A surviving American crewmember told his interrogators that he was part of a secret U.S. contra aid program. In early November, just as American voters returned control of the Senate to the Democrats, Iran disclosed the secret arms sales and chortled that the American weapons had not gone to "moderates," but to anti-U.S. Khomeini loyalists who had hoodwinked the Reagan administration.

President Reagan, Casey, North, and other participants tried desperately at first to cover up the scandal by shredding incriminating documents and lying about their actions to the press, the public, and eventually to Congress and a special prosecutor. Despite compelling evidence of his active role in the scheme, Reagan insisted that he knew virtually nothing about any arms-for-hostages deal or illegal funding of the contras. But the public no longer believed him and by December 1986 Reagan's approval rating plummeted from 67 percent to 36 percent

Under tremendous pressure to come clean, and with the active involvement of Nancy Reagan and aide David Abshire, the president appointed a blue-ribbon inquiry panel chaired by former senator John Tower. After hearing misleading and confused testimony from Reagan (who first admitted, then denied, then said he could not recall trading arms for hostages and diverting funds), the Tower Commission concluded in its February 1987 report that the Iran arms sales had devolved into a sordid ransom scheme designed to illegally fund the contras. Reagan's actions ran "directly counter" to his public promise to punish terrorists.

The report portrayed the president as disengaged, uninformed, and easily manipulated. Reagan sidestepped the criticism by firing many of his aides linked to the Iran-contra scheme (Casey died of a brain tumor in the midst of the scandal) and by giving a speech on March 4, 1987, in which he appeared to accept responsibility without actually doing so. The "facts" might suggest he permitted ransom payments and other illegal acts, Reagan asserted, but in his "heart" he never meant to break the law. Several congressional probes and criminal trials over the next few years added many details to the Iran-contra episode. After Reagan left office, participants in the scheme confirmed that he had approved their actions and impeded full disclosure.

Despite some talk among Democrats of impeachment, Reagan survived the scandal for several reasons. The competing congressional and judicial investigations into Iran-contra often lacked focus. Despite public disappointment in his actions, Reagan retained an important quotient of goodwill. But perhaps the most important reason why the scandal faded was the striking improvement in Soviet-American relations. In 1985, a thaw had begun between Moscow and Washington. By 1987, fundamental changes had occurred inside the Soviet Union and Reagan rushed to embrace them. Ironically, improved relations with the "evil empire" salvaged Reagan's legacy.

Reagan, Gorbachev, and the End of the Cold War

As his supporters saw it, even if the president erred in "small things" like Iran-contra, he steered a true course on the most important issue, engineering the demise of the "evil empire." As Alaska senator Ted Stevens remarked at Reagan's funeral in June 2004, the Soviet Union was "winning the Cold War" at the time of his inauguration in 1981; just eight years later, it was poised to collapse. In contrast to this claim of cause and effect, most historians dispute the assertion that communism was on a victory roll in 1981 and that Reagan's policies led directly to Soviet collapse a decade later.

The Reagan administration's relationship with the Soviet Union started badly in 1981 and soon got worse. At his first press conference, Reagan condemned détente and branded Soviet leaders as liars and criminals committed to world domination. It would no longer be business as usual with Moscow. Yet even as he spoke, Reagan asked Secretary of State Haig to inform Soviet ambassador Anatoly Dobrynin that his statement was not meant to offend anyone, "but was just an expression of his deep convictions." Dobrynin responded that the clarification "only made things worse."[50]

This pattern persisted into Reagan's second term. The president pushed a military buildup and challenged Soviet proxies in the third world. He condemned the Soviet Union as the "focus of evil in the modern world" and a rotten system ready to be shoved onto the "ash heap of history." Yet Reagan often followed these rhetorical attacks with warm personal letters to Soviet leaders (Leonid Brezhnev, who died in November 1982, and his successors Yuri Andropov from November 1982 to February 1984, Konstantin Chernenko from February 1984 to March 1985, and Mikhail Gorbachev after March 1985) containing pleas for cooperation and understanding. Reagan told aides that if he could only talk one-on-one with Soviet leaders, he could convince them of America's good intentions and show them the correct path to change.

In spite of this professed interest in dialogue, Reagan shunned meeting any Soviet official before February 15, 1983, when Secretary of State Shultz brought Ambassador Dobrynin to the White House for an impromptu chat. Reagan took the opportunity to voice concern for seven Siberian Pentecostals holed up in the U.S. embassy in Moscow since 1978. Two months after this conversation, the religious dissidents were permitted to emigrate. In July, Reagan responded by agreeing to sell the Soviets $10 billion worth of grain over the next five years, despite his pressure on the Europeans and Japanese to stop their trade with the Kremlin.[51]

This typified the contradictions in Reagan's Soviet policy, especially those related to nuclear weapons. Reagan sometimes spoke of nuclear war as the biblically prophesied battle called Armageddon. Yet he took office determined to expand America's arsenal of 10,000 or so atomic bombs to counter the Soviet's 8,000 weapons. After starting a rapid buildup, Reagan called for abolishing nuclear weapons in 1984. By 1987 he and his Soviet counterpart agreed to do away with a small number of nuclear-tipped missiles. Yet after this start he spurned further efforts by Gorbachev to slash nuclear arsenals.

Frosty relations with the Soviets hit new lows during 1983. On September 1, U.S. intelligence officials learned from electronic intercepts that a Soviet fighter plane had the previous day downed Korean Airlines Flight 007, which was carrying 269 people (including a member of Congress) and had strayed into Siberian airspace near a missile test site while flying from Anchorage to Seoul. Evidence later confirmed that a navigational error caused the intrusion. Soviet spokesmen (uncertain of the facts and preoccupied by the disabling illness of Communist Party chief Yuri Andropov) first denied that the shootdown had occurred, then insisted that the airliner was a spy plane and a legitimate target. From intercepted messages, U.S. intelligence analysts realized that the Soviets sincerely, although mistakenly, believed KAL 007 had been on a spy mission. In spite of this confusion, Reagan quickly condemned the attack as an intentional, unprovoked massacre and a "crime against humanity."[52]

Also in September 1983, the imminent deployment of American Pershing II and cruise missiles to Western Europe infuriated Soviet leaders. Reagan insisted that the new missiles only redressed earlier Soviet deployment of similar weapons capable of hitting Western Europe. From his hospital bed, Andropov condemned the missile transfer as dispelling "any illusion" that Reagan favored improving ties. The Soviets canceled a planned round of disarmament talks. In October 1983, after the U.S. invasion of Grenada, the Soviet press compared Reagan to Hitler, a madman "making delirious plans for world domination." That December, when U.S. forces conducted a secret war game called Exercise Able Archer, Soviet intelligence warned Andropov that the simulation might be a cover for a real nuclear attack, perhaps requiring a Soviet first strike.[53]

Reagan viewed the deployment of U.S. intermediate-range missiles in Europe, along with the Grenada invasion and arms buildup, as great achievements. At the same time, pollsters warned him that nearly half of all Americans voiced concern over rising tensions with the Soviet Union. Secretary of State Shultz and Robert McFarlane, who replaced the more conservative William Clark as national security adviser in October 1983, along with Assistant Chief of Staff Michael Deaver and Nancy Reagan, urged the president to take a more conciliatory approach. He agreed and on November 11 in a speech in Japan declared, "my dream is to see the day when nuclear weapons will be banished from the face of the earth." In December, at Shultz's prompting, the president sent a personal letter to Andropov. Then, on January 16, 1984, Reagan made a speech in which he described a coming "year of opportunities for peace." The United States and the USSR should resume a dialogue based on "realism" and a "spirit of compromise." He added a coda about how wonderful it would be if ordinary Russians like "Ivan and Anya" could meet their American counterparts, "Jim and Sally."[54]

Soviet leader Andropov's lingering terminal illness and death on February 9, 1984, precluded a response. His successor, Konstantin Chernenko, held power for barely one year, until March 1985. A plodding party functionary, Chernenko suffered from severe emphysema that limited his activities. The succession of decrepit leaders in Moscow reduced pressure on Reagan to justify to the world his own tough approach.

In the run-up to the 1984 U.S. presidential election, Reagan carefully modulated his anti-Soviet rhetoric, backing off from his early confrontational line. He denied harboring a desire or plan to overthrow the communist regime. "We made it plain we're not out to change" the Soviet system, Reagan declared. "We're certainly not going to let them change ours"; but "we have to live in the world together." This hardly sounded like a man who planned to topple the USSR. Reagan's conciliatory tone, combined with an improving American economy, soothed voters' fears and assured the president's reelection by a landslide in November 1984.[55]

The Soviet-American dynamic changed dramatically on March 11, 1985, when the young (age fifty-four), vigorous, and well-educated Mikhail Gorbachev was chosen by Communist Party officials to lead the Soviet Union. As the best educated, most traveled, most media-savvy, and most articulate Soviet leader since Lenin, Gorbachev impressed all Western leaders who initially met him, including Secretary of State Shultz and British prime minister Thatcher. They (along with an astrologer consulted by the president and first lady) encouraged Reagan to meet Gorbachev.

A "getting-to-know-you" encounter at Geneva in November 1985 proved helpful, even if no formal agreements emerged. Reagan found Gorbachev's openness and lack of doctrinaire rhetoric appealing. During their initial chat, the president startled Gorbachev by breaking into what his aides called his "little green men speech." Achieving peace would be simpler, Reagan explained, "if there was a threat to this world from some other species, from another planet, outside this universe." If so, Soviets and Americans would "forget all the little local differences that we have between our countries and we would find out once and for all that we really are all human beings here on this Earth together." This scenario resembled that of a 1950s film Reagan admired, *The Day the Earth Stood Still.*

It is hard to know what Gorbachev made of this parable, which the president often recited to his own confused aides, but Reagan's easy charm overcame any awkwardness. In any case, Gorbachev enjoyed hearing the president, a former movie and television actor, tell insider stories about Hollywood film stars from the 1940s and 1950s.

The two leaders also broached more substantial issues at Geneva, including the idea of deep cuts in a variety of strategic nuclear weapons. Gorbachev wanted to explore details; but when Reagan insisted that any reduction in nuclear weapons must be linked to a green light for the United States to develop and deploy the SDI antimissile system (despite the clear prohibitions against this contained in the ABM Treaty signed by both countries in 1972), discussion ended. When Gorbachev complained that SDI marked a dangerous escalation of the arms race, Reagan countered with his mantra that the antimissile scheme was a "shield, not a spear."[56]

Reagan's rigidity on SDI puzzled some of his aides as much as it angered Gorbachev since no workable system existed or would likely be developed before a decade or longer. In effect, Reagan's refusal to discuss serious arms reductions until the Soviets consented to American testing and deployment of SDI blocked progress toward Reagan's stated goal of a nuclear-free world.

Gorbachev's desire to end the Cold War stemmed primarily from forces and ideas within the Soviet system. As one of the best informed scholars of the period, Raymond Garthoff, observes, America's so-called victory in the Cold War "came when a new generation of Soviet leaders realized how badly their system at home and their policies abroad had failed." Gorbachev, unlike his predecessors, recognized the "interdependence of the world," the priority of "all human values over class values," and the indivisibility of common security. In spite of later claims by Reagan and his conservative admirers, the Soviets did not "lose" the arms race because of America's faster pace. Gorbachev simply called it off. Reagan had the good fortune—and good sense—to respond to these changes even if he had only a small part in initiating them.[57]

During 1986, Gorbachev, along with his new foreign minister, Eduard Shevardnadze, initiated fundamental changes in Soviet domestic and foreign policy. Gorbachev attempted to save communism by reforming it. He began lifting press restrictions, releasing political prisoners, and easing immigration restrictions. To revitalize the economy, he introduced new market mechanisms. To implement these reforms, the new Soviet leadership sought reductions in global tension and lower arms expenditures along with expanded economic ties to the capitalist world.

Gorbachev's initiatives coincided with American interests but were not forced on him by Reagan.

The length the Soviets were prepared to go became clear as the two leaders met a second time in Reykjavik, Iceland, in mid-October 1986. Gorbachev stunned American delegates by proposing 50 percent cuts in the number of heavy missiles along with substantial reductions in other weapons systems. In turn, he wanted the United States to adhere to the ABM treaty for another ten years, confining SDI to laboratory testing. Reagan again balked.

As proposals flew back and forth, the teams of negotiators proposed deeper and wider cuts of nuclear arsenals. Critical issues remained unclear, including the future status of British and French missiles, the size of conventional armed forces, and whether the reductions applied only to delivery systems (such as missiles and planes) or to nuclear weapons themselves. Reagan ultimately proposed eliminating *all* nuclear weapons (not just delivery systems). Gorbachev agreed, so long as the United States did not deploy an antimissile system for at least a decade. Declaring that he had "promised the American people" he would "not give up SDI," Reagan broke off discussions and returned home.[58]

In retrospect, Reagan's supporters assert that the president's unbending commitment to SDI broke Gorbachev's resistance and set the stage for a general Soviet retreat, but this assertion is difficult to confirm. Both Gorbachev and Reagan's aides, including George Shultz, recognized that SDI deployment was, at best, many years away. Why would Reagan not move now toward meaningful disarmament and proceed with SDI *research* that Gorbachev did not oppose? Conversely, why did Gorbachev give up the chance to win arms cuts he desperately wanted when all he had to do was give an approving nod toward a largely imaginary SDI system that fascinated Reagan? The rigidity displayed by both leaders doomed the summit. Many of Reagan's more conservative aides were privately relieved by the failure to reach a deal since few of them understood exactly what the president thought he was agreeing to.

Three weeks after the confused Reykjavik summit broke up without agreement, the Iran-contra scandal erupted. In the simultaneous November 1986 congressional election, Republicans lost control of the Senate. As the scandal deepened and as the public expressed growing disillusionment with the president's behavior and ability, Reagan worked to salvage his presidency by replacing many of his hard-line anti-Soviet advisers with more moderate strategists. Frank Carlucci took over as national security adviser from the disgraced John Poindexter; former senator Howard Baker replaced the abrasive Don Regan as White House chief of staff; FBI director William Webster took charge of the CIA from the ailing William Casey; a few months later Caspar Weinberger resigned as defense secretary. Carlucci then took over the Pentagon post, opening the NSC slot for General Colin Powell. Secretary of State Shultz, long the lone voice advocating negotiations with Moscow, now enjoyed the backing of a much more pragmatic and like-minded group.

During 1987, events pushed both Gorbachev and Reagan toward a more cooperative relationship. When Gorbachev's economic and social reform program ran into roadblocks created by Communist Party bureaucrats, the Soviet public grew frustrated at his inability to deliver a better life. Gorbachev hoped to slash Soviet defense spending (an estimated 25 percent of gross national product, as compared to 3 percent in the United States) to free resources for economic restructuring. He hoped that democratic reforms would both mobilize support for his leadership and win concessions from Washington.

To this end, in 1987 Gorbachev proposed to Reagan a deal eliminating most intermediate-range nuclear missiles, while leaving the Americans wiggle room for SDI. The Soviet leader's proposal reflected advice given him by the recently freed dissident, physicist Andrei Sakharov. The "father of the Soviet H-bomb," who had become a peace activist, convinced Gorbachev that SDI either would not work or could be easily and cheaply overwhelmed. Because it posed little threat to Soviet security, Sakharov argued persuasively, it should not bar arms reduction agreements between the two superpowers. Shultz and other moderates now advising Reagan saw this new Soviet stance as something of a lifeline for a president floundering in the Iran-contra scandal and watching his public approval ratings falling sharply. Congressional Democrats had already blocked increased defense spending requested by the White House, halted aid to the contras, and balked at endorsing Reagan's view that the ABM treaty could be reinterpreted to permit SDI testing and deployment. In the spring Gorbachev suggested sharp cuts of both long- and short-range missiles, with an understanding that the United States could conduct limited SDI research. Yet, once again, Reagan refused to accept any limits on SDI. Defense Secretary Weinberger actually proposed accelerated SDI development to counter what he called a growing Soviet threat.[59]

Frustrated by Reagan's refusal to compromise, Gorbachev went forward according to his own road map and simply ignored the issue of

SDI. In late 1987, he announced he would pull all Soviet forces out of Afghanistan. He followed this declaration by endorsing peaceful solutions to armed conflicts in Nicaragua and Africa. These actions paved the way for a treaty signed by Gorbachev and Reagan in December 1987 that eliminated the entire arsenal of both powers' intermediate-range nuclear forces (INF). Although the INF treaty reduced only about 4 percent of the tens of thousands of nuclear weapons contained in the overall U.S. and Soviet arsenals, it marked the first time the two rivals had agreed to completely eliminate a class of weapons.

Unfortunately, the INF treaty represented the first and last arms reduction agreement of the Reagan administration. Gorbachev hoped to build on the momentum by moving toward big reductions in long-range missiles and even offered to ignore future U.S. testing of SDI, which he told Reagan he now considered more a waste of money than a threat. The president who seemed so self-assured when confronting hostile Soviet leaders appeared to lose his bearings when he got yes for an answer. During Gorbachev's December 1987 visit to Washington for the INF treaty signing, the Soviet leader and the president met in the cabinet room. When Gorbachev described an opportunity to further reduce nuclear arsenals and cooperate in areas like Africa, Latin America, and Afghanistan, the president appeared confused. To the visible fury of Shultz, Reagan responded to the proposal by telling off-color anti-Soviet jokes. Shultz took the president aside to berate his "terrible performance." White House chief of staff Baker and Shultz agreed to closely monitor Reagan's future discussions with foreign leaders, sensing that his mental faculties were no longer adequate for conducting negotiations. By this point more Americans (65 percent) held a favorable view of Gorbachev than of Reagan (61 percent). When *Time* selected its "Man of the Year" for 1987, Mikhail Gorbachev graced the magazine cover.[60]

Reagan's passivity during his final months in office impeded efforts to build on the INF treaty and on Gorbachev's desire to move quickly beyond the Cold War. During 1988, the president simply coasted toward retirement. When he stepped down, over 80 percent of Americans expressed a favorable view of the Soviet leader (as compared to 70 percent for Reagan) and only 30 percent still called the Soviets "the enemy." Yet, instead of encouraging Gorbachev's democratic reforms and efforts to build international cooperation, in public and private venues Reagan took to boasting that his hard line had forced a Soviet retreat. He appeared to lose interest in further antinuclear initiatives when some of his conservative supporters complained about his misguided "rush to disarm." When Soviet forces departed Afghanistan ahead of their announced schedule, Reagan spurned Gorbachev's call for Washington and Moscow to jointly support a new moderate regime in Kabul. Instead, despite earlier pledges to halt weapons aid once Soviet forces left Afghanistan, the United States continued to arm Islamist fighters seeking to control the country. Many of these extremists later formed the core of the Taliban.[61]

In June 1988, the president traveled to Moscow for something like a victory lap. In a remarkable photo op, the old Cold Warrior spoke to a crowd while standing on Lenin's tomb. When asked by an American reporter how he felt about visiting the "evil empire," Reagan answered, "I was talking about another time, another era." But when Gorbachev again sought to involve him in a discussion of broader disarmament as well as cooperation to resolve lingering regional disputes, Reagan did little more than smile for the cameras.

Legacies

Near the end of the Reagan era, Mikhail Gorbachev sardonically asked the president's sixth national security adviser, Colin Powell, "What are you going to do now that you've lost your best enemy?"[62] Powell, like Reagan, had no easy answer.

By the time the Soviet Union dissolved in December 1991, new threats had emerged in the post–Cold War world. George Kennan, the architect of containment, spoke to this fact in an opinion piece he published in the *New York Times* on October 28, 1992. It was "simply childish," Kennan asserted, to say that Reagan's policies achieved victory. The United States had not "won" the long struggle that cost both sides so dearly. Each bore responsibility for its inception and duration. Politicians should pause before patting themselves on the back.

The premier novelist of the Cold War, John Le Carré, offered a similar caution against American "triumphalism." Master spy George Smiley, Le Carré's fictional narrator, observes, "We won. Not that the victory matters a damn. And perhaps we didn't win anyway. Perhaps they just lost. Or perhaps without the bonds of ideological conflict to restrain us any more, our troubles are just beginning."[63]

In the wake of the Reagan presidency, the United States faced a range of unanticipated challenges. The anti-Soviet fixation of the 1980s did not prepare the nation for emerging challenges such as the rise of

Islamist-inspired terrorism, the proliferation of nuclear weapons among rogue states, America's growing dependence on imported energy, and the accelerating loss of manufacturing jobs to China and other developing nations. Reagan's strident campaign to delegitimize the Soviet Union carried over into an erosion of faith among Americans in the legitimacy of their own government.

Under Regan's successor, President George H.W. Bush, the nation's foreign policy centered on arranging a soft landing for the Soviet collapse and on creating an effective coalition to force Iraqi soldiers out of oil-rich Kuwait. In 1993, after Republicans in Congress blamed President Bill Clinton for the deaths of a few dozen U.S. soldiers engaged in humanitarian relief work in Somalia, he hesitated to undertake new foreign interventions. The United States, like most of the world, ignored the Rwandan genocide of 1994 and hesitated to intervene in the ethnic slaughter that afflicted the former components of Yugoslavia during much of the 1990s. When Clinton finally convinced NATO to launch an air offensive against Serbian forces carrying out ethnic cleansing in Kosovo in 1999, he did so over the objections of most congressional Republicans.

As a presidential candidate in 2000, George W. Bush appeared to strike an isolationist tone, stressing his opposition to using American power and armed forces to implement what he descriptively called "nation-building" in poor countries. Yet the 9/11 terrorist attacks within the United States in 2001 pushed the Bush administration in new directions. Several of the diplomatic and military advisers Bush came to rely on, including Vice President Dick Cheney, Defense Secretary Donald Rumsfeld, Pentagon aides Paul Wolfowitz and Richard Perle, diplomats Elliott Abrams and John Negraponte, had been influential figures in the Reagan administration. These so-called neoconservatives, or neocons, had encouraged Reagan's early confrontational policies with the Soviet Union; covert military intervention in Afghanistan, the Middle East, Africa, and Central America; and strong support for Israeli hard-liners in their confrontation with Palestinians. Most were sidelined after the Iran-contra scandal and played marginal or no roles in the first Bush and the Clinton administrations. In 2001, several assumed important positions in the newly elected Bush administration but, as a group, they gained dominance only after the events of 9/11. Their influence showed clearly in the language employed by Bush during 2002 and 2003 when, updating Reagan's reference to the Soviets as an "evil empire," he described Iraq, Iran, and North Korea as an "axis of evil."

Collectively, these neocons advocated increased defense spending, the rapid deployment of a missile defense system, preemptive military strikes against hostile regimes or terrorist groups, contempt for the United Nations, and the overthrow of the Saddam Hussein government in Iraq. Following the terrorist strikes of September 11, 2001, George Bush relied heavily on the advice of this group and implemented most of their policies. In fact, the Iraq war was a pillar of Reagan-era neocons who served Bush. Recalling how freedom rapidly took root in Eastern Europe once the Soviet yoke disappeared, they predicted that deposing Saddam would similarly transform Iraq into a showcase of democracy in the Middle East. Their theories, like their enthusiasm, proved a poor predictor of actual events.

2

The Economic Costs
of Reagan Mythology

John W. Sloan

Myths can be defined as traditional stories or fables that explain phenomena through the feats of gods and heroes.[1] The functions of myths are to clarify the past and serve as a guide for the future. Myths contain moral truths meant to be learned and followed. Many conservative writers use the mythic mode, a tone that reflects awe and reverence, when discussing Ronald Reagan. They describe him as an extraordinary man engaged in performing heroic deeds. In the conservative view, his words—even his jokes—reflect the wisdom of eternal truths that had been violated in the decades before Reagan assumed the presidency in January 1981; his life and rhetoric provide lessons for individuals and the nation to emulate.

Conservative writers portray the mythical Reagan as the lone warrior, dedicated to fulfilling visions based on traditional American values.[2] There was no need for him to study the details of issues because he intuitively understood the big picture: liberal policies had weakened the nation, and conservative policies would strengthen it. He was politically courageous because he was willing to defy the conventional wisdom of liberal experts with his simple but profound ideas and unwilling to compromise his conservative goals. Reagan had a lucid, precise vision of what needed to be done to get the United States back on its traditional track, and he never wavered in his pursuit of conservative programs that would guarantee a prosperous and moral future.

There is a need to deconstruct the mythology of the Reagan presidency. The deconstruction of Reagan does not mean the destruction of his reputation and achievements. It does suggest a scholarly commitment to finding the truth about the Reagan administration, regardless of whether the evidence supports or refutes the ideological beliefs of liberals or conservatives. The real world often has a way of surprising the expectations of mice, men, and, especially, ideologues. We need to cut through the mythological mist that obscures the successes and failures of Reagan's economic policies. The perpetuation of several Reagan myths is likely to cause policy makers to misdiagnose the nation's problems and limit our search for solutions. In brief, ideologically derived images of the Reagan presidency can prevent us from understanding how his presidency really operated and provide a dangerous model for presidential behavior.

A Demythologized View of Reagan's Economic Policies

On January 20, 1981, Ronald Reagan became president with the goal of fulfilling the most ambitious policy agenda since Franklin Roosevelt's New Deal in 1933. Reagan's political project was both to destroy the liberal regime created by Roosevelt and advanced by Lyndon Johnson's Great Society and to construct a conservative replacement. The Reagan administration failed to eliminate most liberal programs and was not successful in passing constitutional amendments outlawing abortion, allowing prayer in public schools, or requiring a balanced budget. However, as I argued in my book *The Reagan Effect,* it did succeed—partly by design, partly by compromise, partly by muddling through—in creating a conservative regime that was capable of promoting long-term economic growth with low inflation.[3] The malaise and stagflation of the 1970s were replaced in the 1980s by an adaptive economy that generated millions of new jobs and discredited the thesis that the United States was a declining superpower.

By design, Reagan was committed to large tax cuts, and much of his political success can be attributed to that fact. The origin of this commitment for Reagan was not philosophical study; he was receptive to the supply-side reasoning that lower tax rates would stimulate economic growth because it was compatible with his Hollywood experience. He often repeated the anecdote that, after World War II, he made only four movies a year because his income from those four alone placed him in the top tax bracket of 91 percent. The highly progressive tax rates created a disincentive to make more movies.[4] These high rates also caused Reagan to develop a visceral dislike of taxes and the Internal Revenue

Service, which he disdainfully called his "senior partner." This animosity toward income taxes made Reagan a different kind of tax cutter than many supply-siders. While supply-siders believed that reducing the top rates would significantly increase savings and investment, Reagan was committed to slashing everyone's tax rates.

Reagan's belief in and commitment to tax decreases were demonstrated in his speeches. For him, government was essentially a wasteful tax spender that—with the exception of national defense—did little good. In 1958, he warned that the graduated income tax had the potential to tax the middle class out of existence and thus bring about socialism.[5] In a 1964 speech for Senator Barry Goldwater, he erroneously claimed, "No nation has ever survived a tax burden that reached a third of its national income."[6] Both as governor of California and as president, Reagan liked to picture himself as a hero protecting taxpayers from the voracious appetites of tax-spending bureaucrats. His speeches attacked both the debilitating effects of the progressive income tax on incentives to work, to save, and to invest as well as its ability to finance an ever-expanding federal government. As a presidential candidate in 1980, Reagan accepted the most sanguine predictions of the supply-siders, namely, that a three-year cut in tax rates would stimulate productivity, increase revenues, and reduce budget deficits.[7] In 1984, three years after Congress had passed Reagan's tax cut and the nation was faced with massive budget deficits, the president resisted the efforts of Martin Feldstein, chair of the Council of Economic Advisers, and David Stockman, director of the Office of Management and Budget, to support tax increases. Reagan, basing his words on a supply-side myth, asserted, "There has not been one tax increase in history that actually raised revenue. And every tax cut, from the 1920s to Kennedy's to ours, has produced more." Feldstein immediately dashed off a brief history of tax revenues before and after tax increase and concluded that "*every* increase in tax rates was followed by a rise in tax revenue [emphasis in original]." For good measure, Feldstein looked at the huge tax increase during World War II and concluded: "There is no evidence that the rising tax rates were incompatible with increased real GNP [gross national product]."[8]

Two experts on tax policy, W. Elliot Brownlee and C. Eugene Steuerle, argue that, "during the late 1970s, Reagan discovered that dismal economic conditions were creating a breeding ground for a popular revolt against government and especially against the tax system."[9] Changes in the tax rate structure from 1960 to 1980 had given the supply-side philosophy a populist appeal that Reagan was able to exploit brilliantly. As Thomas Edsall points out, in 1960, the progressivity of the tax system was targeted at the top 5 percent of the population. Only 3 percent of married couples earned as much as $15,000 a year in 1961; over 80 percent of the population made less than $8,000. For the bulk of the population, there was little or no tax disadvantage in receiving a major salary increase or from inflation-induced bracket creep. As Edsall explains, "Between 1960 and 1979, however, the median family income grew from $5,620 to $19,684, in part from inflation and in part from real increases in spendable income. What had been a statistically exceptional income in 1960 became in 1978 the median income. . . . As a consequence of this process, the sharply rising marginal rates that had been targeted at the very affluent in the early 1960s—while most of the population faced what amounted to a flat tax—became a system in which the vast majority of taxpayers faced sharply increasing marginal tax rates as their income grew."[10] By 1980, about half of all income tax returns were reflecting higher marginal rates than in 1960. Brownlee and Steuerle add that, "the 'bracket-creep' in income tax rates often became 'bracket-leap.' At the extreme, some upper-middle-class people saw their marginal federal income tax rate almost double from 22 percent to over 40 percent, while their state and local income tax were also growing much faster than their incomes. And it was not just the rich and middle class who were affected. Many lower-income people, especially those with dependents, had to pay income tax for the first time as the value of their personal and dependent exemptions and the effective tax-exempt level of income eroded."[11] Thus, by 1980, the average taxpayer was paying rates that had been designed (by Democrats!) to tax the rich. This situation was exacerbated by inflation-driven bracket creep; inflation soared from 7.7 percent in 1978 to 13.5 percent in 1980.

Reagan's response to the stagflation of the late 1970s was two major tax bills: the Economic Recovery Tax Act (ERTA) of 1981 and the Tax Reform Act (TRA) of 1986. ERTA was the top policy priority during the first year of Reagan's presidency; its passage, which fulfilled one of his major campaign promises, helped to establish his credentials as a leader who knew how to wield presidential power successfully. In 1981, Reagan began his presidency by rolling over Congress with the passage of ERTA and $35 billion worth of budget cuts. The passage of the TRA in 1986 was the administration's major domestic success in Reagan's second term. Although both bills lowered tax rates, the philosophy underlying each of them was quite different. What conservative mythmakers also overlook is that the success of the administration's economic policies was not dependent on a strict adherence to Reagan's visions—popularly known as "staying the course"—but instead relied on such course corrections as tax increases and a major change in monetary policy.

ERTA was the largest tax cut in the history of the United States. It provided a tax cut of over $37 billion in 1982, increasing to about $267 billion in 1986, for a total five-year revenue loss to the Treasury of $750 billion. The rates on individual income taxes would be reduced by 5 percent on October 1, 1981, 10 percent on July 1, 1982, and 10 percent on July 1, 1983. The top tax rate was sliced from 70 percent to 50 percent on January 1, 1982. For individuals, ERTA included marriage penalty relief, indexing (beginning in 1985, there would be annual adjustments in personal exemptions, zero bracket amounts, and income brackets to offset bracket creep caused by inflation), a drop in the capital gains rate from 28 to 20 percent, and wider margins on tax breaks for home sellers. Businesses received generous depreciation write-offs for buildings, equipment, and vehicles; they also benefited from investment tax credits ranging from 6 to 10 percent and reductions in the corporate tax rates. Savings incentives were increased by authorizing banks and savings institutions to issue one-year savers' certificates and by expanding the number of people eligible to participate in IRA programs. The threshold for estate taxes was raised from $175,625 to $600,000, and the tax exemption for gifts from parents to children or between spouses was expanded to cover gifts up to $10,000 per year (previously $3,000). There were also numerous benefits for the oil industry and oil royalty owners. In brief, ERTA had two provisions that raised revenues and thirty that reduced them.[12]

ERTA was supported by a philosophy that held that it was good to riddle the tax code with tax expenditures (also known as tax loopholes) aimed at benefiting savers and investors. Supply-siders argued that the liberal regime's "income tax penalizes savers by taxing twice income earned and saved while taxing only once income earned and spent, and that the income tax taxes capital income twice—at both the corporate and the individual level. To redress this imbalance, conservatives often wanted to lower further the effective tax rate on capital income and supported the adoption of new tax expenditures favoring capital."[13] Since Reagan had publicly supported tax expenditures during the 1970s and even made the incredible argument that few loopholes benefit the wealthy, he did not object when business lobbyists like Charles Walker filled ERTA with tax breaks.[14] But C. Eugene Steuerle, a tax expert who worked in Reagan's Treasury Department, did object since he believed that the multitude of tax expenditures in ERTA violated rational tax principles. In Steuerle's words, "Unlike many previous subtle and hidden attempts to grant special favors, here was a wide open and readily acknowledged attempt to create zero or negative effective rates on an economy-wide scale. Many taxpayers began to believe that the government favored the purchase of shelters. . . . The government seemed to claim, at least temporarily, that what was good for the shelter market was good for the country."[15] It was not.

For Steuerle, the most significant component of ERTA was the requirement that the fourteen tax brackets, the personal exemption, and the standard deduction be indexed, which meant annually adapted to the inflation rate after 1984. No longer would the perverse incentive exist where the federal government would be rewarded with increased revenue because of inflation. "By 1990," according to Steuerle, "the adjustment for inflation alone was estimated to have reduced receipts by over $57 billion relative to an unindexed tax code."[16] The irony here is that indexing was not part of Reagan's initial tax bill; Congress added it.

The passage of ERTA did not produce the economic miracles predicted by Reagan and his supply-side advisers. In September 1981, the economy nose-dived into a recession, unemployment rose to 10.7 percent in late 1982, revenue declined, and the budget deficit rose from $73.8 billion in 1980 to $207.8 billion in 1983. Public perceptions that the Reagan administration was promoting tax breaks for the rich and budget cuts for the poor hurt both the president and the Republican Party. In 1982, Reagan's public approval ratings declined to about 35 percent, and the Republicans lost twenty-six House seats in the congressional elections. The public's fear of budget deficits forced the administration to consider painful alternatives, such as tax increases and cutting the growth in mandatory entitlement spending for popular programs such as Social Security and Medicare. The Reagan administration's response to the policy dilemma, in Steuerle's words, was not a profile in courage.

> Leadership for the details of initiatives was seldom to be provided by the president and the White House. Real responsibility was to rest with the Republican Senate and with a commission [headed by Alan Greenspan] designed to deal with the possibility that the social security program might have insufficient funds to meet its obligations. Within the administration,

political forces were split: some proclaiming the need for further tax cuts, and others working to try to reduce the deficit. The administration would waffle in its role. It did not want to take responsibility for any tax increases, but some of its members wanted deficit reduction that might include some tax increases. The president's public position was that he opposed all taxes, but he eventually accepted many increases. In this situation, the visible leadership role was often left to others.[17]

It was *not* part of Reagan's original design that he would feel compelled to accept several tax increases in order to respond to the unexpected (for him) deepening deficits. Jitters about budget deficits and concerns about saving Social Security caused Congress to pass tax increases in 1982, 1983, and 1984, all of which were signed into law by Reagan. The most significant bill was the Tax Equity and Fiscal Responsibility Act (TEFRA) of 1982, which was designed to raise $98.3 billion over three years and thus effectively regain one-fourth of the tax revenue lost in 1981. Congress passed TEFRA in August 1982 largely because of the political skills of Senator Robert Dole, who was then chair of the Senate Finance Committee. This was the first significant tax increase enacted by Congress during an election year in peacetime since 1932.[18] In July 1984, Congress passed and Reagan signed another bill, the Deficit Reduction Act (DEFRA) of 1984, which raised taxes by closing sixteen loopholes. "Taken together," according to Brownlee and Steuerle, "TEFRA and DEFRA raised revenues on the average of $100 billion per year at 1990 levels of income. Increases this big had never been enacted except during major wars."[19] Obviously, there had been a retreat from the thinking that had supported ERTA in 1981. The White House spin machine did not call these changes tax increases; it labeled them revisions in the tax code.

The retreat continued as the administration prepared for the president's 1984 State of the Union address, which fortuitously launched a set of forces that brought about major tax reform in 1986. In December 1983, Treasury Secretary Donald Regan, with the information that many corporations were able to avoid federal taxation by taking advantage of tax loopholes, tried to convince the president to advocate tax reform in his State of the Union address. The tax system needed to be fundamentally changed because it was too complex, too unfair, and too restrictive on economic growth.[20] James Baker and Richard Darman, the president's top pragmatic advisers, wanted Reagan to stress deficit reduction and were skeptical about the appeal of tax reform in the upcoming presidential election. But Baker and Darman were fearful that Walter Mondale, the likely Democratic presidential candidate, might focus his campaign on the unfairness of the tax code. Hence, early in 1984, Baker, mistakenly believing that Mondale might champion the Bradley-Gephardt tax bill, which would simplify the tax code and lower tax rates, suggested that Reagan direct the Treasury Department to develop comprehensive tax reform legislation. Accepting Baker's advice, the president in his State of the Union address ordered Secretary Regan to conduct a study of tax reform and report back to him in December 1984. This maneuver essentially neutralized tax reform as an issue during the 1984 campaign. During the campaign, the focus was on the fact that Mondale wanted to raise taxes and Reagan did not.

After the 1984 election, the Treasury Department presented its recommended tax reform bill (called Treasury I) to the president. Treasury I, skillfully prepared by the neutrally competent bureaucrats in the department, recommended the elimination of 38 of 105 tax expenditures. Early in 1985, Chief of Staff James Baker and Treasury Secretary Donald Regan switched jobs. In reviewing Treasury I, Treasury Secretary Baker and his deputy, Darman, decided that the proposal would have to be revised to make it more politically feasible before it could be introduced to Congress. This was done, and President Reagan presented his tax bill (known as Treasury II) to Congress in late May 1985. Unlike the situation in 1981, Reagan could not steamroll his opponents in 1985, but he was able to impose a major rule: any bill would have to be revenue-neutral. That is, any new tax bill would have to raise the same amount of revenue as the existing tax law. According to tax policy expert John Witte, "Revenue neutrality had an important direct effect. It repressed the temptation to add revenue—losing tax breaks because it provided the committee chairs with a simple rule—for every break proposed, the proponent had to find an offsetting revenue gain."[21] Still, each house of Congress significantly modified the bill; the result was not simply a fulfillment of Reagan's vision. The Tax Reform Act was finally passed by Congress and signed by President Reagan on October 22, 1986.

The philosophy underlying the TRA was that, in broadening the tax base by reducing the number of tax loopholes, the government could significantly lower tax rates. TRA's chief selling point was that it reduced the fourteen rate brackets to two rates of 15 and 28 percent, with a complicated surtax that placed some upper-middle-class families (with joint income between $71,900 and $149,250) in a 33 percent bracket. An estimated 80 percent of American families fell into the 15 percent bracket. Thus, as Michael Boskin pointed out, "The top marginal tax rate in the personal income tax will have gone from 70 percent in 1980 to 28 percent by 1988, an astounding reduction, making the *top* marginal tax rate in the United States lower than the *bottom* marginal tax rate in many countries."[22] By almost doubling the exemptions for self, spouse, and dependents, TRA removed approximately 6 million poor from the tax rolls. Democrats supported this provision for its fairness and Republicans for being pro-family. TRA eliminated the preferential treatment of capital gains income by raising the tax rate from 20 percent to the top individual rate of 28 percent. For many individuals, being able to take the standard deduction, which had been significantly raised, greatly simplified the filing of their tax returns. It was estimated that about 60 percent of all Americans paid slightly lower taxes (a few hundred dollars per year) because of this reform law, and another 25 percent paid what they had been paying before. The remaining 15 percent faced a relatively small tax increase.[23]

The TRA was an outstanding example of reform legislation because it overcame politicians' natural inclinations to reward special interests (especially those groups who provide generous campaign contributions) with tax breaks. According to Witte, "TRA dwarfs any of the three prior peacetime reform acts. . . . Seventy-two provisions tightened tax expenditures, including fourteen that involved complete repeal, a figure approximately equal to the total number of tax expenditures that had been repealed from 1913 to 1985. . . . The initial estimates of revenue gains from tightening and closing tax expenditures were $324 billion over five years."[24]

The most surprising feature of the TRA was that, between 1986 and 1991, it shifted an estimated $120 billion of the tax burden from individuals to corporations. As explained by Boskin, "This occurs despite the fact that the basic corporate tax rate is being reduced from forty-six percent to thirty-four percent because of a very substantial increase in the corporate tax base, achieved through the elimination of the investment tax credit, much slower depreciation, and a stiff alternative minimum tax for corporations (to insure that no corporation that reports current profits to its shareholders will avoid paying taxes)."[25] The playing field for corporations may have been leveled by this tax reform, but it was now also more expensive to play.

The chief player in promoting the unlikely passage of the TRA was Ronald Reagan. He placed tax reform on the policy agenda by making it the symbol of his "second American Revolution" in his 1985 State of the Union address. Reagan had the chameleon-like capability of identifying with and appealing to those who felt that taxes were too complex, those who felt that taxes were unfair, those who felt that the rich were not paying their fair share, and those who felt that taxes impeded their chances to move up. One of his major public relations achievements was to plant the idea that the progressive income tax was elitist and that flatter rates were egalitarian because they provided more opportunities for more people to do better. The president's tax reform was portrayed as pro-fairness, pro-family, and pro-growth; it epitomized Reagan's conservative populism.

Reagan saved the bill in November 1985 when House Republicans were repelled by the modifications imposed by Dan Rostenkowski's Ways and Means Committee. He helped create an atmosphere in which no one wanted to appear responsible for killing the reform proposal. Witte suggests, "Reagan's support of tax reform amplified the unique political jockeying that the issue stimulated in both parties. In a bizarre political reversal of 1981, in deficit-plagued 1985 and 1986, tax reform acquired the same political momentum as wholesale tax reduction and loophole expansion had in 1981."[26] As Steuerle explains, "Once it became clear that an administratively feasible system could be designed that would lower rates and eliminate shelters, remove the poor from tax rolls, and treat individuals with equal income more equally, no one wanted to be known as the person who stood in the way of this effort and caused it to fail."[27] In a major study of the passage of the TRA, two *Wall Street Journal* reporters concluded that "Reagan wanted to go down in history as the president who cut that top tax rate at least in half, from 70 percent to 35 percent or lower. If abandoning tax breaks and raising corporate taxes were the price he had to pay to achieve that goal, so be it."[28]

However, despite Reagan's enthusiastic speech making in support of the TRA, it is likely that he was not knowledgeable about the major provisions in his own proposal. In an interview following his 1985 State of the Union address, the president revealed that he did not understand that his Treasury II proposal included a 36 percent increase in corporate taxes.[29] In Albert Hunt's words, "The president's ignorance of the specifics of his own proposal was startling; throughout, he misrepresented or misunderstood the measure's tax increase on business, but President Reagan's attachment to lower rates was real and his commitment to the concept of tax reform was even more powerful than his ignorance of the details. He never quite convinced the public, but his political persona

Table 2.1

The Reagan Administration's Economic Record

	GNP (billions of 1982 dollars)	Percent change from preceding year	Gross private investment (billions of 1982 dollars)	Unem- ployment rate	Federal yearly change in CPI	Federal budget deficits (billions)
1980	3,187.1	−0.2	509.3	7.0	13.5	−73.8
1981	3,248.8	1.9	545.5	7.5	10.3	−78.9
1982	3,166.0	−2.5	447.3	9.5	6.2	−127.9
1983	3,279.1	3.6	504.0	9.5	3.2	−207.8
1984	3,501.4	6.8	658.4	7.4	4.3	−185.3
1985	3,618.7	3.4	637.0	7.1	3.6	−212.3
1986	3,717.9	2.7	639.6	6.9	1.9	−221.2
1987	3,845.3	3.4	669.0	6.1	3.6	−149.7
1988	4,016.9	4.5	705.7	5.4	4.1	−155.1
1989	4,117.7	2.5	716.9	5.2	4.8	−153.4

Source: Economic Report (1991).

and communication skills commanded such respect that they scared off a lot of potential opponents."[30]

By focusing on reducing the top rates on individual income taxes, Reagan failed to see how philosophically inconsistent ERTA and TRA were. Whereas ERTA had created a number of tax expenditures to encourage savings and investment, the TRA emphasized leveling the playing field by eliminating or reducing seventy-two tax expenditures. Tax breaks that had been designed to encourage specific economic activities were now removed because it was felt that they distorted the choices taxpayers and businesses were making. The irony of the 1986 tax reform was that it was designed to close many of the loopholes in ERTA. Witte wryly concludes, "Ronald Reagan thus has the unique historical position of supporting both the largest tax reform and the largest anti-tax reform legislation in the history of the United States."[31]

The Consequences of Reagan's Economic Policies

The statistical evidence summarizing the Reagan presidency does not support the conservative assertion that there was a "Reagan revolution"; it does bolster the proposition that he had a good, solid economic record (see Table 2.1). When Reagan and his supply-side supporters came to power, they euphorically expected that their tax cuts would both stimulate the economy and shrink the federal government by reducing its funding. Once in office, however, confronting a Democratically controlled House throughout the 1980s, they found it was more politically feasible to cut taxes than to cut expenditures. In 1980, federal taxes constituted 19 percent and federal expenditures 21.4 percent of the gross domestic product (GDP). By 1989, taxes constituted a slightly lower 18.5 percent, while expenditures remained at 21.4 percent of a considerably larger GDP.[32] Despite Reagan's rhetoric opposing big government, he eliminated very few programs and succeeded only in slowing the growth of federal spending (adjusted for inflation) from about 4 percent a year during the Carter years (1977–1981) to about 2.5 percent during the 1980s.[33]

Since the 1981 tax cuts did not produce a supply-side miracle, the result was annual budget deficits leading to massive increases in the national debt. Reagan had promised to balance the budget by 1984, but in his eight years in office, he never proposed a balanced budget. During the 1980s, the U.S. national debt increased from $914 billion to $2.6 trillion. The total national debt accumulated under the nation's first thirty-nine presidents more than doubled under its fortieth, Ronald Reagan. When Reagan was inaugurated, it cost the Treasury $71 billion a year to service the national debt; when he left office, debt service had soared to over $150 billion annually. Not until 1995 would the budget deficit, measured as a percentage of the GDP, fall below the level Reagan inherited in 1981.

The Reagan administration predicted that the passage of the $750 billion tax cut in August 1981 would generate rational exuberance in financial markets. Supply-siders believed that even before the tax reductions took effect, the depressed stock and bond markets would quickly react with brisk rallies. Instead, defying these ideological forecasts, both markets declined in August and September 1981. Rather than enjoying a burst of prosperity, Reagan found himself challenged by a recession.

The 1981–1982 slump was the eighth recession the United States had suffered since the end of World War II. There were over 25,000 business failures in 1982, the second highest number since 1933, during the Depression. In November 1982, more than 9 million Americans were unemployed, a number that would climb to a peak of 11.5 million in January 1983. Whereas the seven postwar business cycles before 1982 averaged an unemployment rate of 7.1 percent at their troughs, the eighth cycle hit an unemployment rate of 10.8 percent at the end of 1982. About 2.3 million manufacturing jobs were lost in the recession, which fueled fears about the deindustrialization of the United States.

Reagan handled this trial by recession fairly well. When Murray Weidenbaum, the chair of the Council of Economic Advisers (CEA), told Reagan in late July 1981 that a recession was about to begin, the normally amiable president reacted with a cold stare of disbelief.[34] By October, he admitted publicly that the economy was suffering from a "slight recession," but he predicted a fast recovery if we had the courage to "stay the course" and continue his policies. While supply-siders and Treasury Secretary Regan blamed the recession on Federal Reserve Board chair Paul Volcker's "excessive" tightening of the money supply, the president did not. He viewed the recession as stemming from the fact that his original supply-side proposal for cutting taxes by 10 percent for three successive years beginning on January 1, 1981, had been delayed and watered down. Reagan had unshakable beliefs that shielded him from doubts about the efficacy of his policies.

As economic conditions deteriorated in 1982, Reagan played the role of cheerleader, encouraging citizens not to lose faith. He condemned the media for emphasizing pessimistic stories, which he believed were delaying the recovery. In his 1982 economic report to Congress, Reagan declared, "I am convinced that our policies . . . are the appropriate response to our current difficulties and will provide the basis for a vigorous economic recovery this year. It is of the greatest importance that we avoid a return to the stop-and-go policies of the past. The private sector works best when the Federal Government intervenes least. The Federal Government's task is to construct a sound, stable, long-term framework in which the private sector is the key engine to growth, employment, and rising living standards."[35] In public speeches, Reagan depicted his administration as the "cleanup crew," tidying up the mess caused by a forty-year "nonstop binge" (a significant metaphor for the son of an alcoholic). From his perspective, this recession provided conclusive evidence that the economic policies of the previous presidencies did not work. He exhorted Americans to increase their savings rate by two percentage points, which would add about $60 billion a year to the nation's capital pool to combat high interest rates and to finance investments, mortgages, and new jobs. Reagan assured the nation that his policies were based not on "quick fixes" but on dealing with the "root causes" of the economic problems and that by taming inflation, which eventually would lead to unemployment if unabated, he was constructing a recovery that was "built to last."[36]

The recession helped the Democrats pick up twenty-six seats in the

House of Representatives in the 1982 congressional elections, thus ending Republic aspirations to control both chambers during the 1980s. Reagan's public approval ratings declined from a high of 67 percent in April 1981 to the mid-30s in early 1983. But exit polls in the 1982 elections indicated that voters were more likely to blame the Democrats rather than Reagan for economic problems.[37] Historian Alonzo Hamby suggested that "it was a measure of the depth of public dissatisfaction with Carter and the Democrats that Reagan was able to survive the worst economic trough since the Great Depression with little damage."[38] Lou Cannon wrote, "Later in his presidency, after Reagan had become a remote and disengaged monarch, first-term aides would recall the grim months of recession as if they were a golden age. They would remember Reagan scoffing at his critics and the polls and defiantly proclaiming that he would 'stay the course' with his economic program. 'The greatest show of his leadership was then,' said speechwriter Bentley Elliott."[39]

The irony of this episode, as will be explained later, is that the success of the Reagan administration's economic policies was not due to "staying the course" but changing it significantly in the summer of 1982.

The political success of the Reagan administration was largely based on its economic performance. As indicated in Table 2.1, the economy began a long-lasting recovery from the recession in 1983, with the GNP increasing 3.6 percent in that year and a whopping 6.8 percent during the presidential election year of 1984. From 1983 to 1990, the economy grew at about 3.5 percent a year, and the GNP expanded by 32 percent. The Dow Jones industrial average went up 32.8 percent in Reagan's first term and 71 percent in the second. From 1982 to 1989, the Standard and Poor's index of 500 stocks went up almost 300 percent. Reagan had fulfilled his 1980 campaign promise to rejuvenate the economy.

The most remarkable attribute of this period of economic growth was its durability. It lasted ninety-two months, which was more than twice the average length of expansions since 1945 although it was exceeded by the 106-month growth period from February 1961 to December 1969, which was partly fueled by the Vietnam War. A new and more resilient economy emerged in the 1980s, one that was able to grow despite fears raised by budget and trade deficits, by the 508-point drop in the Dow Jones index in October 1987, and by all the technological changes that seemed to be accelerating. During the 1980s the United States underwent a metamorphosis from a manufacturing economy to a more flexible information-based, service-providing economy created by computer, revolutions in shipping (UPS), just-in-time ordering, efficiency-minded reorganizations and plant closings, outsourcing, and the increasing use of temporary workers.

Supply-siders exaggerate the success of Reagan's economic policies. They evaluate Reagan's performance using data from 1983 to 1990, blaming the 1981–1982 recession on President Carter and the 1990–1991 recession on President Bush's decision to raise taxes. In 1990, Martin Anderson declared, "We don't know whether historians will call it the Great Expansion of the 1980s or Reagan's Great Expansion, but we do know from official economic statistics that the seven-year period from 1982 to 1989 was the greatest, consistent burst of economic activity ever seen in the United States."[40] The evidence demonstrates, however, that the economy performed better in the 1960s, under the Keynesian policies of Kennedy and Johnson, than in the 1980s. In the 1960s, the GDP expanded 52.8 percent; in the 1980s, 34.7 percent. In the 1960s, worker productivity improved 31.8 percent; in the 1980s, 15.6 percent. In the 1960s, median family income (adjusted for inflation) increased by 39.7 percent; in the 1980s, it increased by only 4.3 percent.[41] In terms of annual GDP growth, presidents Truman (5.9 percent), Kennedy/Johnson (4.9 percent), and Johnson (4.4 percent) had better records than Reagan (2.3 percent in his first term and 3.2 percent in his second).[42] What made Reagan's economic record look so good was comparisons to the last two years of the Carter presidency.

The political success of the Reagan presidency was largely dependent on the 18 million new jobs that the American economy produced during the 1980s. In 1980, over 99 million Americans had jobs, and the unemployment rate stood at about 7 percent; by 1990, almost 118 million workers were employed, and the unemployment rate had dropped to 5.4 percent.[43] Apologists for Reagan skip over the point that 1.9 million jobs were lost between April 1981 and November 1982 and stress that in the twenty-seven months after November 1982, 7.6 million jobs were produced. Conservatives also neglect to report that the economy produced more jobs in the 1970s and 1990s than in the 1980s.[44]

The Reagan presidency had less success in increasing Americans' propensity to save and invest than it did in providing jobs. In 1981, the administration's program for economic recovery stressed that, in contrast to the inflationary, demand-led expansions of the past, growth in the 1980s would be based on the supply side of the economy. Increases in savings and investment would allow the economy to flourish without anxiety about capacity-induced inflation pressures. Administration supply-siders such as Norman Ture predicted that tax cuts would increase gross private savings (composed of personal and business savings). Personal savings as a proportion of disposable personal income were projected to rise from an average of 5.4 percent in 1977–1980 to 7.9 percent in 1986. Business savings, which generally account for slightly more than two-thirds of total private savings, were forecast to climb above the 17 percent of GDP rate that had been maintained since 1956.[45]

These goals were not achieved. Personal savings, instead of rising to 8 percent of disposable income, fell and averaged only 4.5 percent during the 1980s. Gross national savings declined from 19.2 percent of the GDP in 1980 to 15.6 percent in 1989.[46] From 1971 to 1980, the net national savings ratio averaged 8.9 percent of the GDP; from 1981 to 1988, it averaged only 3.7 percent.[47] Changes in the tax code did not cause the American people to give up their inclination to consume. Instead, we continued to be a buy now, pay later society. Consumer debt, as a proportion of personal income after taxes, climbed from 62.7 percent in 1970 to 74.9 percent in 1980 and reached 96.9 percent in 1990.[48] Increased consumption accounted for over two-thirds of the growth during the economic expansion from 1982 to 1990. Fortunately for the administration's pro-growth policy, however, the capital-short, consumption-driven U.S. economy was bailed out by an unforeseen boost in foreign investment, which was attracted to our low-inflation, high-interest safe haven.

But the Reagan presidency was dependent on more than its ability to promote economic growth; sustainable growth would require a monetary policy to prevent inflation. When Reagan became president in 1981, according to George Will, "prudent people were worried that inflation was the systemic disease of democracies. That is, democracies could not resist deficit spending, and would use inflation as slow motion repudiation of their deficits. Furthermore, democracies, with low pain thresholds, could not endure the pain involved in wringing inflation from the system."[49] By the time Reagan left office, inflation was considered a manageable problem. Credit for taming inflation should be shared between the administration and Paul Volcker's Federal Reserve Board. During the decade, the consumer price index (CPI) was reduced from 13.5 percent in 1980 to 4.1 percent in 1988. Inflation averaged about 3.6 percent between 1983 and 1989, which helped to lower interest rates. Since inflation has corrosive effects on both the value of money and incentives to promote economic growth, lowering inflation rates was an essential ingredient in promoting long-term expansion. In the past, growth periods have been derailed by severe inflation, which have led to the imposition of high interest rates by the Federal Reserve. Cannon correctly argues, "The long period of low inflation had a stabilizing effect in the United States and was of enormous political benefit to Reagan. . . . [T]he Reagan-Volcker legacy of treating inflation as Public Enemy No. 1 . . . may well prove the most enduring and popular of Reagan's conflicting economic legacies."[50] In brief, confronting inflation was as important for Reagan's success as dealing with unemployment was for Franklin Roosevelt's.

The administration's initial anti-inflation strategy was based on Milton Friedman's theory, which assumed that there was a direct relationship between the quantity of money in the economy and the level of output. When the money supply decreased, there was a recession; when it expanded moderately, there was sustainable economic growth; and when it grew too fast, there was inflation. Obviously, the correct choice was to have the Federal Reserve provide a slow, steady increase in the supply of money, but this alternative, so easy to select in theory, proved impossible to implement in practice.

Monetary policy proved to be essential for Reagan's success in the 1980s, but not as originally planned by the administration. The key strategist in the battle against inflation was Paul Volcker, who had been appointed chair of the Federal Reserve Board in 1979 by President Carter. Just as Reagan was attempting to restore confidence in the presidency, Volcker was trying to restore confidence in the Federal Reserve Board after its failure to control inflation in the late 1970s. During Volcker's Senate confirmation hearings, he labeled himself a "pragmatic monetarist," which signaled that he would not rigidly adhere to Friedman's doctrine. Volcker strongly believed that inflation was a growing menace that threatened the health of the economy and that only a hard-nosed monetary policy could free us from its insidious effects. He saw that inflation had become deeply entrenched in our economic expectations and behavior. By the end of the 1970s, the inflationary process was feeding on itself and distorting economic incentives. In Volcker's words, "Too much of the energy of our citizens was directed toward seeking protection from future price increases and toward speculative activity, and too little toward production."[51] Unlike Reagan, he felt that only a prolonged and painful process would be successful in combating an inflationary system that had grown too large to be harnessed by moderate means. The repeated failures since the late 1960s had bred skepticism as to whether policy makers had the knowledge, commitment, and courage to subdue inflation.

With inflation appearing out of control, Volcker led the seven-person Federal Reserve Board into a Friedman-inspired monetary experiment in October 1979. Instead of trying to control interest rates, the Federal Reserve would set specific supply goals and employ its authority over bank reserves. The shift in focus from interest rates to restricting the growth of the money supply was designed to signal markets that a new and far more serious effort was under way to combat inflation. The plan was to establish a target for M1 (currency in circulation plus checking accounts) growth and then "hit" it by manipulating bank reserves. Bank reserves are influenced by the activities of the Federal Open Market Committee (FOMC), which meets eight times a year. The FOMC is composed of the seven members of the Federal Reserve Board and five of the twelve Federal Reserve Bank presidents. It always includes the president of the Federal Reserve Bank of New York; the other members rotate. The FOMC determines open market policy—that is, it decides whether to buy or sell government securities (bills, notes, and bonds). FOMC directives to ease or tighten the money supply are implemented by the Open Market Desk of the Federal Reserve Bank in New York. To stimulate monetary growth, the Federal Reserve buys government securities; to tighten the money supply, it sells government securities. As Albert Rees explains, "When the Federal Reserve buys securities, it pays for them by creating deposits for the sellers in the Federal Reserve Banks; these deposits serve as additions to reserves for commercial banks. The added reserves permit commercial banks as a group to expand their loans and deposits by a multiple of the new reserves; this multiple is the inverse of the reserve ratio. For example, if reserves of ten percent are required against all deposits, an additional dollar of reserves could ultimately support $10 of additional deposits."[52] When the Federal Reserve sells government securities, it has the opposite effect.

With inflationary expectations so embedded in pricing and wage behavior and with politicians refusing to make the compromises necessary to prevent soaring budget deficits, Volcker knew that it would take a long period of tight money to slow down inflation. Not operating in a rose-colored campaign mode, Volcker never promised a quick or easy victory over inflation. As the Federal Reserve tightened the money supply and allowed interest rates to float, the economy slowed down, and then went into a severe recession in the autumn of 1981. High interest rates cause business failures and rising unemployment rates. Volcker's cure for inflation seemed to be causing more pain than the disease. Inevitably, a wide variety of congressional leaders—House Majority Leader Jim Wright, Congressman Jack Kemp, Senator Ted Kennedy, and Senator Howard Baker—condemned Volcker. Supply-siders complained that, while Reagan's plan had called for the automatic and gradual decrease in the rate of money growth over a four- to six-year period, Volcker's policy had "delivered 80 percent of this reduction in money growth in the first year—an extraordinarily recessionary policy."[53] Milton Friedman accused the Federal Reserve of sabotaging his policy, not because it did not know how to bring about stable monetary growth, but because most of its policy makers were "unreconstructed Keynesians" who were more interested in controlling credit than in providing steady monetary growth. The results, according to Friedman, were erratic monetary growth and interest rates.[54]

Within the Reagan administration, Volcker was reprimanded by Treasury Secretary Donald Regan and Treasury Undersecretary Beryl Sprinkel (a former student of Milton Friedman), who vaguely threatened the Federal Reserve Board by talking about administration studies that would reduce its independence. Yet Reagan generally supported the Federal Reserve Board. In Volcker's words,

> President Reagan must have received lots of advice to take on the Fed himself, but he never did despite plenty of invitations at press conferences. . . . I never saw him often, as I had Mr. Carter, nor did I ever feel able to develop much personal rapport or indeed much influence with him. He was unfailingly courteous, but he plainly had no inclination either to get into really substantive discussions of monetary policy or, conversely, to seek my advice in other areas. But I had the sense that, unlike some of his predecessors, he had a strong visceral aversion to inflation and an instinct that, whatever some of his advisers might have thought, it wasn't a good idea to tamper with the independence of the Federal Reserve.[55]

As inflation rates declined in 1982, Volcker acknowledged that stabilizing prices during the most severe recession in forty years was not a great victory. The real challenge was to promote a noninflationary recovery and sustained economic expansion. His goal was to use monetary policy to make the 1980s a "mirror image of the 1970s," reversing the debilitating trends of the past decade.[56] By preventing inflation that typically becomes a problem after four or five years of economic expansion, he aimed to prolong the growth phase of the business cycle.

In July 1982, after establishing its credibility as an inflation fighter, and with Congress about to pass a $98 billion tax increase that would lower future budget deficits, the Federal Reserve began to loosen the money supply by raising money targets. On July 19 it lowered the discount rate from 12 to 11.5 percent. The FOMC also announced that it was temporarily suspending money supply targeting; Volcker was ending the monetarist experiment and allowing the money supply to expand at a faster pace in order to lower interest rates. In August 1982, Reagan signed the TEFRA. On August 17, the Dow Jones index experienced its highest single-day rise in its history (38.81 points) to finish at 831.24, with a near record trading volume of over 92 million shares.[57] Between July and October 1982, the Federal Reserve permitted the M1 money supply to grow by 15 percent. It appears that an implicit compromise was negotiated—the administration accepted a tighter fiscal policy in exchange for the Federal Reserve's pursuing a looser monetary policy. Volcker had both initiated and ended Friedman's monetarist experiment and set the stage for a long period of noninflationary economic growth. In August 1982, the stock market began the longest bull market in U.S. history.

The 1980s were not kind to Friedman's theory. After the Federal Reserve tightened the money supply in 1981 and 1982, it allowed M1 to grow by 11 percent in 1983 and 7 percent in 1984. James Alt reports, "For the 1980s as a whole, M1 growth [was] just under 8 percent per annum, two points higher than in the 1970s, while M2 growth averaged just over 8 percent, the same as it was in the 1970s."[58] Despite this growth in the money supply, inflation rates in the 1980s were considerably lower than in the 1970s. In 1982, Friedman forecast a rise in inflation followed by a recession in 1984, predictions that were embarrassingly wrong.[59] Benjamin Friedman (no relation to Milton) pointed out "since 1980 the relationship between money growth and the growth of either income or prices in the United States has collapsed. . . . Further, because the mid-1980s brought both the fastest money growth of the postwar period and the greatest *dis*inflation, the correlation between money growth and price inflation calculated in the way recommended by Milton Friedman (using two-year averages to smooth out short-run irregularities, and a two year lag between the money growth and the inflation) is now *negative* for postwar samples including this decade."[60]

Friedman's theory was also wounded by the fact that, with the government deregulating the banking system, it became more difficult, perhaps impossible, for the Federal Reserve to control the growth of the money supply. There were months when the Federal Reserve sought to restrict M1, yet it expanded. At other times, the opposite occurred. Arthur Schlesinger lampooned Friedman's monetary experiment by writing, "Friedmanism, with its spurious claim to precision, received its obituary from Sir Ian Gilmour at last year's Conservative Party conference when, evoking Oscar Wilde's description of fox hunting as 'the unspeakable in pursuit of the uneatable,' he called monetarism 'the indefinable in pursuit of the uncontrollable.'"[61]

Milton Friedman's theory concentrated on the slow, steady growth of the supply of money and considered interest rates and unemployment of secondary importance. Since most of the public has no understanding about the quantity of money but *is* affected by interest rates and unemployment, it is not surprising that political support for Friedman's monetarism disintegrated during the early 1980s. After Volcker ended Friedman's monetarist experiment in 1982, Reagan reappointed him chair in 1983. (Could his reappointment have been part of the price for Volcker's agreeing to loosen the supply of money in July 1982?) Thus, Friedman experienced the reward of winning the Nobel Prize for economics and the humiliation of having his theory proven unworkable when applied to national monetary policy.

The success of Volcker's pragmatic, discretionary monetary policy, as opposed to Friedman's automatic monetary policy, played an indispensable role in supporting Reagan's presidency. Volcker helped Reagan construct a vital component of a new policy regime that was able to promote economic growth that was less susceptible to inflation than the Keynesian-inspired one. Because the old system based on the Phillips curve (whereby the Federal Reserve allowed inflation to inch up in order to bring down unemployment) had broken down by the end of the 1970s, a new strategy was required in the 1980s. Instead of using Federal Reserve control over the money supply to balance levels of inflation and unemployment, the new system stressed the strategic importance of preventing inflation. In permitting interest rates to rise and fall more freely, the Federal Reserve stabilized the business cycle by inhibiting both overheating and stalling. The new strategy held that sustained economic growth was derived from an effective anti-inflationary policy, which meant hiking interest rates in response to the first signs of inflation. Given the rigidities of the budget and the frequent gridlock between the president and Congress, fiscal policy was playing a declining role in controlling inflation and in stabilizing the business cycle. With the federal government, private corporations, and individuals piling up debts and with increasing international mobility of private capital seeking higher interest rates, the role of monetary policy had grown rapidly and become preeminent in promoting prosperity. It could fuel investment and growth without expanding federal spending. By 1986, even a Keynesian economist could write, "the monetary policy of the Federal Reserve has become the dominant instrument of macroeconomic management. If any fine or coarse tuning of the economy is done, it's the Fed that calls the tune, through its control of money and interest rates. After all, Chairman Volcker and his colleagues can make nine or ten moves a year. The budget makers in the executive and Congress can make only one, and in recent years their procedures, politics and conflicts have become so complex that national economic prospects and strategies play little role in the outcome."[62] In brief, the chairman of the Federal Reserve has become the most important economic policy maker in the United States.

The success of Volcker's policies causes some problems for Reagan's ideological supporters. First, Volcker was originally appointed chair of the Federal Reserve by Carter, the personification of failed liberalism. After much debate within the Reagan administration, Volcker was reappointed in 1983 but was replaced by Alan Greenspan in 1987. Second, Volcker's monetary policy, which was largely followed by his successor, was a national policy, formulated by a centralized political institution that successfully muzzled inflation without inhibiting job creation and economic growth. After the economy recovered from the 1981–1982 recession, the Federal Reserve's goal was to navigate an overheated economy into a "soft landing," allowing growth to remain positive, thus avoiding a "hard landing," which would cause the economy to contract. Such metaphors sounded suspiciously like the Keynesian concept of "fine-tuning" the business cycle that had so offended conservatives in the 1960s. The Volcker-Greenspan success story weakens the conservative assertion that discretionary government policies cannot improve market outcomes. Most important, the record indicates that Volcker did more of the "heaving lifting" in fighting inflation than Reagan. While the president cut taxes and ran large budget deficits, Volcker bore the political heat of keeping interest rates fairly high. The self-serving conservative narrative is that Volcker's policies caused the recession, and Reagan's policies brought about noninflationary economic growth. Reagan deserves credit for not attacking Volcker during the dark days of the 1981–1982 recession and for reappointing him in 1983, and Volcker was clearly the architect of the anti-inflationary strategy that has proved so essential in promoting a prolonged economic expansion.

President Reagan made major contributions to the creation of this policy regime, which overcame the dilemmas of stagflation and demonstrated that the economy could enjoy a long period of economic growth while avoiding inflation. His tax cuts for both individuals and corporations stimulated the prosperity that, except for a short, mild recession in 1990–1991 continued into the 1990s. However, this framework for economic growth was not simply a function of fulfilling Reagan's original visions in 1980. Contrary to Reagan's speeches and conservative myth spinners, the president's success was not based on "staying the course"; rather, it derived from his skill in shifting policy direction while maintaining rhetorical consistency. By 1982, it was apparent that there was a fundamental incompatibility between Reagan's fiscal and monetary policies. An implicit compromise was arranged whereby the administration accepted a tighter fiscal policy by acquiescing to tax increases, and Volcker's Federal Reserve Board agreed to implement a looser monetary policy. Volcker ended Friedman's experiment in 1982, was reappointed chairman in 1983, and then skillfully directed monetary policy to constrain inflation. Low levels of inflation were an essential ingredient in prolonging the growth stage of the business cycle. There was nothing courageous in Reagan's signing several tax measures that had been negotiated by a Congress anxious to reduce budget deficits, thus lowering the threat of inflation and freeing Volcker to loosen the supply of money and credit.

Mythical Lessons

The challenge for conservatives has been to explain the economic phenomena of the 1990s and George W. Bush's first administration (2001–2005) from the perspective of the eternal truths that Reagan had rediscovered. Conservatives had no problem in accounting for the failure of George H.W. Bush (1989–1993). He was viewed as more of a country club Republican than a Reaganite. In 1980, he had called Reagan's proposed supply-side tax cut "voodoo economics," and so, in 1990, it came as no surprise that he violated his "Read my lips" campaign promise and signed a major tax increase to reduce the budget deficit. Bush suffered the inevitable and proper fate: the economy declined into a recession, the budget was not balanced, and he was defeated by Bill Clinton in 1992.

Conservatives disregard the facts that Bush felt he had to sign the tax increase because of the budget constraints imposed by the Gramm-Rudman law, a bill signed by Reagan in 1985; he had to deal with the enormous expenses of bailing out hundreds of savings and loan institutions that had been deregulated during the 1980s, a problem that Reagan refused to face; and he had to make sure the military was adequately funded to fight the Gulf War to liberate Kuwait.

A second challenge for conservatives was to explain—or to explain away—Bill Clinton's economic successes. As a "new Democrat," Clinton was persuaded by his moderate advisers (Lloyd Bentsen and Robert Rubin) to raise taxes in order to lower the budget deficit, which was about $290 billion in 1992. While Clinton was not happy to be reneging on his campaign promise to cut taxes for the middle class and respond to the needs of bondholders, a Republican constituency, Bentsen and Rubin, plus Greenspan, convinced him that progress toward balancing the budget would significantly lower interest rates, promote long-term growth, and place more dollars in the public's pockets than a tax cut would. When Clinton signed his deficit reduction package on August 10, 1993, conservatives, particularly outraged by the hike in the top individual income tax rate to 39 percent, predicted that the legislation would cause great harm to the economy. Newt Gingrich proclaimed, "I believe this will lead to a recession next year. . . . This is the Democratic Machine's recession and each one of them will be held accountable."[63] Robert Rubin, Clinton's second secretary of the treasury, summarizes what happened during the rest of the 1990s:

> The 1993 deficit reduction program was a test case for supply-side theory. Instead of the job losses, increased deficits, and recession the supply-siders predicted, the economy had a remarkable eight years—the longest period of continuous economic expansion yet recorded. Unemployment fell from more than 7 percent to 4 percent, accompanied by the creation of more than 20 million new private-sector jobs. Inflation remained low while GDP averaged 3.5 per annum. Productivity growth averaged 2.5 percent a year between 1995 and 2000, a level not seen since the early 1970s. Poverty rates went down significantly, including among Blacks and Hispanics, and incomes rose for both higher and lower earners. For the first time in nearly 30 years, the budget balanced in 1998.[64]

The fact that the world did not conform to their ideological predictions did not faze most conservatives; they disingenuously shifted their argument that Clinton's tax increase would cause a recession to one that proposed that the prosperity of the 1990s had nothing to do with Clinton's policies and everything to do with the continuation of Reagan's. Republicans insisted that Reagan's policies were totally responsible for the economic growth of the 1980s, but that Clinton's programs had no effect on the record-breaking economic growth of the 1990s.[65] Ideology blinded many conservatives from seeing that both Bush and Clinton, in confronting the painful issues of the failing savings and loans and the rising structural budget deficits, had provided key pegs for the record-breaking expansion of the 1990s and demonstrated more political courage than had Reagan. The movement toward a balanced budget soothed financial markets and allowed the Fed to keep interest rates at low levels.

Adhering to the Reagan mythology has helped George W. Bush politically but will severely damage the nation economically. This Bush administration, influenced by senior political adviser Karl Rove, has been guided by conservative myths that budget deficits can be ignored, that tax reductions mainly targeted for the benefit of the rich will stimulate the economy, that economic growth will inevitably solve budget problems, and that the senior Bush presidency committed an unforgivable sin by agreeing to a tax increase in 1990 and thus suffered the inevitable result of a recession and an electoral defeat. Conveniently forgotten are the three tax increases that Reagan signed in order to reverse the soaring budget deficits caused by the overly generous tax cuts enacted in 1981. The result was a negative transformation in the fiscal situation from small budget surpluses during the last three years of the Clinton presidency (obviously constrained by a Republican-controlled Congress) to expanding budget deficits under Bush, including a record high deficit of $413 billion in fiscal year 2004. While Bush promises to slice the budget deficit in half by 2008, few analysts believe that is possible, since the administration is engaged in an expensive war and occupation in Iraq, as well as being committed to an expensive (measured in the trillions) Social Security reform, and since it remains vehemently opposed to tax hikes. After the congressional elections in November 2002, Bush's treasury secretary Paul O'Neill warned at a budget meeting that the federal government was approaching a fiscal crisis; he was abruptly interrupted by Vice President Dick Cheney, who retorted, "Reagan proved deficits don't matter. . . . We won the midterms. This is our due."[66] For conservatives, the mythology of Reaganomics defanged the fear of deficits and freed them from the responsibility of weighing the costs of diminished revenue in proposing tax cuts. Hence, conservative Republicans are as prone to fling tax breaks at problems as liberal Democrats were to throw money at maladies in the 1960s.[67] Operating in this ideological never-never land, Bush can win elections and can steadfastly stay on message in his demands for tax cuts and opposition to tax increases, but neither he nor conservatives can change the laws of math. With Reagan's mythology casting its delusional spell over both the Bush administration and most of the Republicans in Congress, the ability of the political system to deal honestly with budget issues in the foreseeable future appears slight.

Another major cost of the Reagan legacy is that it created a regime that ignores growing disparities in income and wealth in the United States. For reasons that are not entirely clear and subject to fierce debates between liberals and conservatives, indexes of inequality have increased since the 1970s. These changes are altering the nature of the United States from one of the most egalitarian industrialized nations to one of the least. The evidence indicates that the policies of the Reagan administration were not the origin of this growing inequality, but it does suggest that they contributed to that trend. More important, Reagan's policies and rhetoric did nothing to inhibit inequality, and his administration attempted to delegitimize any governmental endeavors to promote equality. By adding barriers to the already Herculean task of helping the poor, Reagan served his partisan purposes but not necessarily the nation's good. The claims of Reagan's supporters that he was a great moral leader can be seriously challenged because he contributed to poisoning the policy milieu against proposals to bring about a more socially just nation.

Reagan championed the conservative idea of individual freedom over equality. Whereas liberals believe that equality and liberty can be reconciled, conservatives do not. Whereas liberals claim that by extending equality a nation is expanding freedom, conservatives assert that attempts to augment equality constitute lethal threats to individual freedom. While liberals tend to think of equality as promoting social justice, conservatives believe that the pursuit of equality brings about stifling uniformity, leveling, and bureaucratic oppression. For liberals, equality is a moral incentive leading to a more socially just society; for conservatives, it is economically counterproductive, politically dangerous, and a demagogic appeal to envy.

Guided by this conservative perspective, the Reagan presidency pursued economic policies that promoted economic growth but did not distribute its gains widely or evenly. Reagan's tax policies mainly benefited the rich, and his budget cuts disproportionately hurt the poor. The unequal results have been extensively documented. In 1991, a Census Bureau study of 24,000 households chosen to be representative of the nation's 92 million households concluded that the wealth of the most affluent Americans increased substantially during the 1980s while the net worth of other citizens barely kept pace with inflation. After adjusting for inflation, the wealth of the richest one-fifth of all households increased 14 percent from 1984 to 1988, while the remaining four-fifths of households did not experience any significant change in net worth.[68]

In 1970, the richest 1 percent of households possessed about 20 percent of the nation's wealth. Twenty-five years later, data from a 1995 Federal Reserve study showed that the wealthiest 1 percent of households—with net worth of at least $2.3 million each—now owned nearly 40 percent of the nation's wealth.[69] In 1980, there were 4,414 millionaires in the United States; by 1987, there were 34,944; by 1994, there were about 65,000.[70] In 1982, there were twenty-one billionaires in the nation; by 1991, there were seventy-one.[71] At the end of the Reagan administration, the top 1 percent of households owned a lopsided proportion of many types of assets: 49 percent of publicly held stock, 62 percent of business assets, 78 percent of bonds and trusts, and 45 percent of nonresidential real estate. Controlling these assets has meant that these affluent households have attracted three-fourths of the gain in pretax income from 1977 to 1989. Sylvia Nasar concludes, "By 1989, the one percent (834,000) households with about $5.7 trillion of net worth was worth more than the bottom 90 percent of Americans (84 million households) with about $4.8 trillion in net worth."[72]

In brief, the Reagan mythology and rhetoric focused more pride on the growing number of millionaires than compassion on the millions of citizens who remain trapped in the prison of poverty.

Conclusion

Since Reagan was the "father" of a regime created in the 1980s, conservatives felt the need to exaggerate his ideological credentials and achievements and erase evidence of his pragmatic capabilities and compromises. They believe that too much of Roosevelt's and Johnson's liberal regime survived and that not enough of Reagan's visions were implemented during the 1980s. In deifying Reagan, conservatives have an unhidden agenda—to commit future Republican presidents and Congresses to fulfilling conservative policy preferences. In their eyes, Reagan's policies worked miracles during the 1980s and should continue to be successful in the twenty-first century.

Reagan's economic policies made a major contribution to overcoming stagflation in the late 1970s and rejuvenating the economy, but the mythologizing of Reagan in the new century threatens to bring about economic disasters. The major cost of Reagan mythology is that it is reducing the rationality of policy makers by limiting the scope of options in dealing with economic problems. By distorting how economic growth and a balanced budget were achieved, goals that were dependent on painful decisions to raise taxes and confront the savings and loan crisis, Reagan mythology is providing false guidelines for dealing with contemporary problems. It is ridiculous to believe that every problem can be solved with a tax break. Moreover, it is time for conservatives to acknowledge that both Reagan's and George W. Bush's tax cuts have not increased the nation's low propensity to save and have widened income disparities.

Reagan's axiom that government is the problem inhibits analyzing when government is the solution, or is part of the solution. (Obviously, the same holds true in examining the role of the market in resolving problems.) Reagan myths make a virtue out of a vice, namely, avoiding expert advice. Bureaucratic expertise in the Treasury Department helped Reagan achieve economic and political success in the Tax Reform Act of 1986. Walter Williams points out, "Even though antigovernmentism did not visibly shrink the size of the federal budget, adherence to the philosophy of limited government produced great damage to the body politic. The simplistic Washington-is-the-problem argument tended to dull the public's awareness of or interest in the serious domestic policy issues that needed to be addressed and blocked any institutional efforts to realistically debate them."[73] The Reagan myths amplify the already present danger that a president operating in the politicized, comfortable cocoon of the White House can be shielded from unpleasant truths. Because these myths are accepted as truth by the conservative movement, responsible behavior in dealing with painful issues by seeking expert advice and by being willing to accept reasonable compromises (as in the Tax Reform Act of 1986) is often condemned and punished. That is not a formula for a successful political system.

The economic costs of Reagan mythology are high because it encourages conservative policy makers to believe in ideologically deduced miracles rather than what is feasible based on empirically derived probabilities. Trust in miracles provides perverse incentives for politicians to avoid confronting painful issues like budget and trade deficits, global warming, the future funding of Social Security and Medicare, and the rebuilding of the gulf coast after the devastating hurricanes of the summer of 2005. Operating under Reagan's shadow, rigid and delusional behavior is defined as moral, and attempts to forge compromises are considered immoral. Reagan's legacy inspires conservatives to champion ideologically based initiatives and condemn both reality-based thinking and pragmatic adjustments. When there is conflict between Reagan's truths and the evidence from math and science, conservatives argue that policy makers should continue Reagan's course and disregard the evidence. Believing that God and history are on their side, American conservatives are absolute in their faith that moral and ideological certainty can change the real world. But it must be noted that, in the past, God and history have been known to confound those who are so rigid in their hubristic beliefs.

3

Reagan and Race

Prophet of Color Blindness, Baiter of the Backlash

Jeremy D. Mayer

> The vast majority of black Americans were suspicious
> of Reagan throughout his campaign and,
> indeed, throughout his presidency.
> —*Stephen L. Carter, Reflections of an Affirmative Action Baby*

Ronald Reagan ended his presidency among the most popular figures in American life. His country embraced the first two-term president since Eisenhower, leaving office with relatively high personal approval ratings. The "Teflon president" had weathered the scandal of Iran-contra and avoided impeachment. Unlike Bill Clinton, who was often less popular than his policies, Reagan was just the opposite: a president who was far more beloved for his avuncular attitude, his personal courage in the face of an assassination attempt, and his sunny disposition than for his policies, his ideology, or even the positive results of his leadership.

Yet Reagan's popularity always carried with it a caveat, an exception, a subset of citizens immune to his prodigious charisma: black Americans. Even as Reagan successfully wooed white Americans (and Americans of other races) to vote for him in record numbers in the electoral landslide of 1984, black Americans remained overwhelmingly opposed to the man and his presidency. It was almost as if there were two Reagans, the upbeat, optimistic, and friendly Reagan that white America saw and the distant, cold, and dangerously insensitive Reagan that black America perceived. The pattern continued long after his presidency. Even as America mourned Reagan's passing in 2004, the crowd at the National Cathedral for his burial was almost entirely white. Television cameras captured few blacks publicly mourning the man many pundits proclaimed the most successful president since Roosevelt, if not one of the two or three greatest presidents in American history.

How can we explain this stark racial division in attitudes toward Reagan in life and in death?

Books written by Reagan's most prominent supporters show an extraordinary absence of discussion of this important question. The silence is deafening. Dinesh D'Souza, in his hagiographic account of Reagan's life, makes no reference to Martin Luther King, Jesse Jackson, Ralph Abernathy, the National Association for the Advancement of Colored People (NAACP), most of the few blacks in the administration (Clarence Pendleton and Clarence Thomas), the battle over the civil rights commission, or even civil rights generally. Affirmative action merits a minor mention in reference to the Reagan administration's attempts to rein it in, but almost every aspect of Reagan's life and presidency that touched on race is ignored.[1]

Former Reagan speechwriter Peggy Noonan similarly ignores almost all racial aspects of his presidency. Like D'Souza, she does not mention Jackson or the NAACP and ignores civil rights almost entirely, except to say erroneously that Reagan agreed with Martin Luther King Jr. While Reagan voiced agreement with King's broad positions long after his death, Reagan was a fierce and frequent critic of the civil rights movement while the man was alive, and, as noted below, even issued an ambivalent statement on the day of King's assassination. While Noonan manages to find space for a famous anecdote about Reagan's racial tolerance during his college years, she avoids almost all mention of race in her discussion of his career and administration. Finally, in a long list of the attacks made against Reagan, she does not include the charge of "racist."[2] True or not, it was often said by prominent blacks and is discussed in every nonpartisan biography of Reagan. Noonan either considered the charge unworthy of refutation or irrefutable.

Similar gaps appear in almost every conservative account of Reagan's life and presidency. It is as if black America's opinion about Reagan, and the issues that divided him from 12 percent of the American population, did not exist. Even Reagan's attorney general, Edwin Meese III, who led the executive agency most concerned with civil rights, cannot bring himself to include more than a smidgen about blacks and civil rights. Meese recounts Jimmy Carter's attacks on Reagan as a racist during the

1980 campaign and mentions how much they angered Reagan, "since anyone who knows him at all knows he is not a racist."[3]

These books, and several other accounts of the Reagan administration, simply ignore the question of Reagan's racial politics, his racial policies, and his racial legacy. But there are reasons why white America and black America perceived Reagan so differently.

To explain the sharp divergence in attitude toward Reagan during and after his life, this essay will explore four aspects of Reagan and race: Reagan the man, Reagan the campaigner, Reagan the policy maker, and Reagan's racial legacy. We begin with Reagan the man, because race and racial issues are far more personal than most in the American firmament. Like those surrounding abortion and homosexuality, race questions frequently lead to investigation of, speculation about, and confrontation over a politician's personal beliefs, history, and character. In the case of Reagan, his biography has played a deeper role than usual in the structuring and selling of his racial views.

Reagan the Man: The Prophet of Color Blindness

Ronald Reagan grew up in and around Dixon, Illinois, a town in which blacks were present but seldom prominent. They could not stay overnight at the hotel, get their haircut downtown, or join the golf club.[4] Although far less open than in much of the South or, indeed, in southern Illinois, racism was part of the fabric of daily life in Dixon. Blacks were few in number and rarely challenged the supremacy of whites. Years later, in the 1980 presidential debate, Reagan made a famous gaffe when he spoke of a time before America even knew it had a racial problem. Yet Reagan's words were surely an accurate description of the mind-set of most of the white residents of Dixon during the early decades of the twentieth century.

Most, but certainly not all, and among the exceptions seem to have been Reagan's parents, Nell and Jack Reagan. Sixty years later, Reagan was still reciting stories of their lack of racial prejudice and openness to blacks in particular.[5] Reagan repeated two anecdotes endlessly whenever the topic of racial discrimination arose. The first dealt with the appearance in Dixon of a rereleased version of the famously racist film about the Ku Klux Klan, *Birth of a Nation*. Reagan, already a devoted film aficionado, was forbidden by his father from attending, because of Jack's aversion to the Klan. Reagan protested that the movie was not about the modern

Klan, but about the historical one, and Jack was supposed to have answered, "The Klan's the Klan, and a sheet's a sheet, and any man who wears one over his head is a bum."[6] In Reagan's memoirs, this incident is the most positive reference he makes to his father, a deeply troubled alcoholic who repeatedly failed at business.[7]

While Jack Reagan's rejection of the Klan might have been motivated by its anti-Catholic stance (Reagan's father, unlike his mother, was Catholic), it seems that Nell and Jack were unusually progressive on racial questions for Dixon and for their time. In the other treasured Reagan anecdote about race, Reagan's college football team found itself in a jam before a road game fifteen miles away from Dixon. The hotel at which they had reservations was segregated, and it refused service to the two black members of the team.[8] The coach decided that the whole team would therefore sleep on the bus. However, Reagan, afraid that this would create resentment against the two black players, making them feel awkward, offered to have the two players stay at his house. The coach had trouble believing that a white family in 1930s Illinois would welcome their son and two black boarders without any advance warning in the middle of the night. But as one of the black teammates attested decades later, Reagan's confidence in his parents was well-founded, and the crisis was quietly avoided.[9] It is difficult for those born later to understand how truly unusual such an act was for a white family at that time, but Reagan's black teammates understood and never forgot.

Years later, when Reagan was a Hollywood actor, he noted with pride in a letter to a friend that he had just finished a movie in which he played a reformist police chief who battled the Klan. Reagan pointed out how proud this would have made his father, another rare positive reference to Jack by his son.[10] Reagan was so certain that he had been raised without prejudice that accusations that he was racist were deeply offensive to him throughout his political career. How many presidents would take the time to handwrite a personal letter to the leader of the NAACP who had accused him of working against the interest of blacks?[11] Reagan did so because he firmly believed that he had not a shred of racism in his character.

In his first campaign for governor of California, Reagan responded with rare public anger to the implication that he was racist. In a debate before a group of black Republicans, Reagan's opponent suggested that Reagan was opposed to blacks, at which point Reagan shouted, "I resent the implication that there is any bigotry in my nature! Don't anyone ever imply that—in this or any other group!" Reagan was so overcome by his anger that he crumpled up his speech and fled the debate, with what appeared to be tears of rage in his eyes, and he was overheard to curse his opponent. It took a few hours before his staff could calm him down enough to return to the venue. This was the only time Reagan lost his temper in the entire campaign.[12]

Reagan's upbringing by racially progressive parents did not just produce a man easily offended by the idea that he was burdened with racial prejudice; it also produced a man with an unusual willingness to express public disdain or anger at black people, particularly black women. Outside the 1968 Republican convention, an aggressive black female protester who pointed out the paucity of blacks in attendance confronted Reagan. Instead of simply ignoring the comment, Reagan got into a shouting match with her in front of reporters. In 1980, while running for president, another shouting black woman confronted Reagan during an ill-fated campaign appearance in the South Bronx. Reagan shouted down the heckler, again in front of reporters, saying "I can't do a damn thing for you if I don't get elected!" The powerful image of an infuriated Reagan shouting at blacks was highly unusual for a white politician.[13] During his time as governor of California, one of Reagan's favorite targets was radical activist Angela Davis, whom he tried to have banned from the University of California system. In the 1976 primary battle with Gerald Ford, Robert Keyes, Reagan's most prominent black supporter during his time in California, ultimately supported Ford out of dismay at Reagan's record on race. When Keyes was on his deathbed, years later, Reagan refused to take his call, a rare act of bitter anger in a man known for his ability to forgive political opponents and for his mastery of the sympathetic gesture.[14] Although these incidents are not particularly numerous in a public career that lasted for twenty-four years, what is surprising is that they occurred at all, given Reagan's publicly sunny disposition and the sensitive nature of race in America during this period.

Ultimately, was Reagan the man a racist? The question is difficult to answer in part because of the multiplicity of definitions of white racism. Certainly, unlike the public George Wallace or the private Richard Nixon, Reagan did not use racist terms for blacks[15] or traffic in odious stereotypes about the black race in general. Reagan's record reveals scant evidence that the man was burdened with racial prejudice on a personal level. Among his intimates, there were no blacks, but not only was this quite common for his era (and, indeed, for American presidents of his generation), but Reagan was famously aloof from even his closest associates. In the 1960s, he once told a joke about Africans and cannibalism, but given the Hollywood milieu and Reagan's gift for telling jokes, it seems a thin reed to build a case against him as a racist. Such jokes were common in the routines of many comedians at the time, black and white.[16]

Yet the question of whether Reagan was a racist or not may be less important than what was Reagan's overall attitude toward race. Reagan seemed to think that race was a problem he had long ago solved in his own heart. Devoid of prejudice (or at least believing himself to be), he argued throughout his career that government efforts to ameliorate racial prejudice were at best far inferior to personal efforts to change hearts. In this way, Reagan was the first prophet of Republican color blindness on race. In the 1950s, the liberal line on race was that the government should step in to prevent official discrimination against blacks. The goal was a color-blind society. As the massive legacy of America's centuries of racism became ever clearer in the 1960s and 1970s, many liberals shifted to a policy of taking cognizance of race in an effort to eradicate racism and its powerful lingering effects. At the same time, many conservatives, gradually rejecting government tolerance of racism, adopted the color-blind rhetoric abandoned by the liberals. Reagan led this shift more than any other political figure. His faith that he lacked racial prejudice allowed him to take positions widely perceived as antiblack without any hesitation. A more introspective or ambivalent white politician might have retreated in the face of nearly unified black anger at his policy positions and campaign tactics. As we shall see, such retreats were almost unknown in the campaigns and policies of Ronald Wilson Reagan. Thus are the character and experiences of the man father to the campaign tactics and governing choices of the politician.

Reagan as Campaigner: The Sunny Salesman of the White Backlash

Reagan's first venture into electoral politics struck conservative Americans like lightning in October 1964. In a nationally televised address, Reagan electrified Goldwater supporters with his powerful, bold rhetoric and extraordinary ease in delivery; but something was missing from the speech. In one of the most racially charged elections in modern American history, in which Goldwater's opposition to the 1964 Civil Rights Act was one of his major appeals for millions of Americans, Reagan said not a word about race or civil rights. Yet surely Reagan must have been aware of how his antigovernment rhetoric would sound in the American South at the time. When Goldwater was defeated in a landslide, the only area of the country where Republicans saw gains at the presidential and congressional levels was the South, where segregation was still widely practiced and wildly popular. Reagan could have easily clarified his position on civil rights in his first major national address or in all the subsequent speeches he made on behalf of Goldwater. Instead, Reagan's speeches tended to avoid race or to point out ways in which legislative efforts to expand civil rights were misguided if well-intentioned.

Following his speech, Reagan quickly became a star in Republican circles, much in demand as a speaker around the country. Encouraged to get into the race for governor of California in 1966, Reagan had to finally address racial issues, as seen in the debate before the black Republicans. Reagan was now firmly on the record as agreeing with Goldwater that the 1964 Civil Rights Act was a mistake. Reagan was also less than fulsome in his praise of the 1965 Voting Rights Act (VRA). In the general election, Reagan ran a radio ad that referred to urban areas as "jungles." In the racially charged era of black riots and in a time when a derogatory term for blacks was "jungle bunnies," the word struck some as a direct appeal to white racism and backlash.[17] Reagan also faced a conundrum when it came to nondiscrimination in housing legislation. Previously he had argued against such legislation at the national level, saying that housing was a state question. But in his gubernatorial campaign, he tried to repeal California's antidiscrimination legislation, seeing it now as a property rights issue: "If an individual wants to discriminate against Negroes or others in selling or renting his house, it is his right to do so." It seemed that no matter how Reagan made the calculation, he was coming out on the antiblack side.[18]

Following his stunning victory in 1966, Reagan was so nationally prominent in Republican circles that he was widely considered presidential timber for 1968. His major rival was Richard Nixon. An internal Nixon memo captures how many saw Reagan: "Reagan's strength derives from personal charisma, glamour, but primarily the ideological fervor of the Right and the emotional distress of those who fear or resent the Negro, and who expect Reagan somehow to keep him 'in his place' or at least to echo their own anger and frustration."[19] Reagan was seen as quite likely to deny southern support to Nixon, where Reagan commanded true passion from whites opposed to black equality. Nixon's staff also considered Reagan the only candidate who could neutralize Alabama's George Wallace, a racist icon contemplating an independent run for the White House in 1968.[20] Ultimately, Nixon had to move far to the racial right to defeat the Reagan challenge. Although it is likely that Nixon would have adopted his southern strategy even if Reagan had never run for president, it might not have been such an anti–civil rights strategy had it not been for Reagan's pressure.

Although brief and unsuccessful, Reagan's little-noted effort at the presidential nomination in 1968 is highly significant for what it says about his campaign appeal. In recent American history, how many other California politicians, after two years in office, could have been expected to rely on solid strength from southern state delegates in a race for a presidential nomination? How did Ronald Reagan, a Californian with no record of animosity toward blacks and no sustained cultural exposure to the American South, become so popular among racially conservative whites in such a brief period of time? In many ways, Reagan was the ideal face for racial conservatism, a movement desperately opposed to black progress but aware that open racism had become anathema to most Americans. Moreover, Reagan had traveled extensively in the South on behalf of General Electric, after his film career ended. Giving these speeches, as well as Republican party speeches throughout the South from 1964 to 1968, taught Reagan very well how to please a southern crowd without crossing lines of open racism. In addition, many of Reagan's other positions, on school prayer, taxes, foreign policy, federalism, and welfare, fit well with southern cultural conservatism. Reagan could allow many white southerners to believe that they had opposed the Civil Rights Act or the Voting Rights Act not because they hated or feared blacks, but because they believed in traditional American values of local government, federalism, and conservatism. This plausible deniability on race was perhaps Reagan's greatest appeal to many racist whites.

It is also important to note Reagan's role as among the most prominent voices calling for strong government action against urban riots, which were highly salient for many northern and southern whites from the mid-1960s to the mid-1970s. In the midst of the rioting era, Reagan made this stunning statement: "The greatest proof of how far we've advanced in race relations is that the white community hasn't lifted a finger against the Negroes."[21] In addition to being factually incorrect (many more blacks were killed by whites in the riots of the 1960s than the converse), praising whites for not taking vengeance against blacks as they had in the recent past was the kind of language that fed the moral legitimacy of the white backlash.

In 1976, Reagan again entered the Republican primaries, this time taking on a sitting president, Gerald Ford. As in 1968, Reagan ran to the racial right of a more moderate Republican. Ford's campaign accurately perceived that Reagan's appeal was deeply related to his positions on race. Ford's pollster found that Reagan supporters were almost indistinguishable in attitude from Wallace supporters.[22] Reagan, like Wallace, endorsed a constitutional amendment to stop school integration through busing. In a nationally televised speech, Reagan linked declines in educational achievement to integration by busing, a popular if little supported contention, which again gave cover to those who opposed liberal solutions for less defensible reasons.[23] In another national television address, Reagan condemned affirmative action and quotas.[24]

In Michigan and Texas, Reagan's campaign relied on former Wallace backers now that Wallace himself had been effectively removed from the Democratic primaries. More than 100,000 brochures were mailed to Wallace supporters on behalf of Reagan.[25] Reagan, like Wallace, also spoke warmly of the apartheid governments of Rhodesia and South Africa, while Ford was cautiously in favor of voting rights for blacks in those countries.[26] In his famous "welfare queen" anecdote, told repeatedly in the 1976 campaign, Reagan echoed Wallace in using welfare to court the white backlash. In Reagan's telling, a woman in the Midwest had used as many as nineteen identities to bilk the government of hundreds of thousands of tax dollars. While Reagan never identified the woman's race, the original story was well known, at least to many in the Midwest. The facts were also well known to many reporters, who pointed out to Reagan that he was greatly exaggerating the case. The actual woman had taken on just two identities, and the amount of money defrauded was exponentially less than Reagan claimed. Reagan continued to give his erroneous version, which was very popular with his audiences.[27] In perhaps the most odious outreach to white racism of the 1976 campaign, Reagan supporters in North Carolina distributed a flyer alleging that Ford was going to put Senator Edward Brooke, a moderate black Republican, on the ticket as his vice president.

Reagan was briefly caught by the shifting tide of American attitudes toward race by one stray comment during the campaign. As he had since the mid-1960s, Reagan cavalierly questioned whether the entire civil rights movement had accomplished much. Given that Reagan was on the record opposing every major plank of that movement, he might have thought that he could get away with it, but the media signaled that such positions could no longer be pitched as nonracial. When challenged about his comments, Reagan retreated into stale platitudes about race.[28] Perhaps more important, the few remaining black Republicans voting in appreciable numbers in the primaries almost uniformly went for Ford over Reagan. In the extraordinarily tight contest, that may have made the difference in the crucial states of Tennessee and Kentucky.[29] Reagan's 1976 campaign was significant for the evolution of racial politics in the Republican Party. It was the last time that black Republicans actually mattered and the first time that former Wallace supporters were crucial. Reagan was central to both developments, as his opposition to civil rights helped drive blacks out and pull backlash whites in.

In 1980, Reagan was positioned as the front-runner from the start of the Republican primary season. But the Reagan of 1980 was radically different in terms of race and campaigning. Reagan simply did not talk about civil rights, busing, or even affirmative action, except when questioned about those specific topics by reporters. According to campaign insiders, the change represented not an alteration in Reagan's views but rather his belief that, as a front-runner, he should focus on issues such as defense policy, taxes, and economic renewal.[30] In one "off-message" moment, Reagan blamed the VRA for the "humiliation" it brought the South. Others might have felt that the American South should have been embarrassed and humiliated by the decades of racist violence and systemic disenfranchisement that made the VRA so necessary, but for Reagan, it was the reporting requirements that were humiliating.[31]

The most unforgettable image of Reagan and race from the 1980 campaign came when he chose to open his campaign at the Neshoba County Fair in Mississippi. This county, and the town of Philadelphia, had famous overtones for both southern whites and civil rights activists, because it was here that voting rights campaigners Andrew Goodman, Michael Schwerner, and James Chaney were kidnapped, executed, and entombed by racist whites in 1964. Reagan's pollster repeatedly asked him to reconsider kicking off his campaign at such a loaded venue, but Reagan got so angry at the suggestion that he threw a folder at his staffer.[32] Not only did Reagan start his campaign in Neshoba, but his speech endorsed states' rights, the very principle advocated by those who murdered the three civil rights martyrs. It is difficult to imagine that Reagan was unaware of what it would mean to both blacks and some whites to endorse states' rights at the Neshoba County Fair.

Yet even the dark moments at Neshoba should not obscure that the Reagan of 1980 was evolving on race, at least in terms of style. Neshoba and the comment on the VRA were far from the central discourse of his campaign, whereas in 1976 busing and racial issues were easily in the top five concerns of his campaign. Two nationally televised speeches of Reagan's in 1976 focused on just these issues. Moreover, as opposed to 1976, Reagan had some significant figures from the black community behind him. Ralph Abernathy, formerly Martin Luther King Jr.'s top aide, and two other minor black civil rights activists openly supported Reagan. Moreover, Reagan spoke to the National Urban League, met with black leaders Vernon Jordan and Jesse Jackson, and even visited an impoverished black neighborhood in the South Bronx. It was at this visit, shortly after the Neshoba kickoff, that an angry crowd of black residents confronted Reagan. Ironically, the only major event designed to show Reagan's willingness to work on issues of black poverty probably helped him shore up his support with the white backlash, since television captured Reagan yelling at poor blacks in anger.[33] But the visit itself, as well as the outreach to black leaders, showed that Reagan at least desired to appear moderate on race. At the Detroit convention, Reagan intervened personally to ensure that the leader of the NAACP was given a prime-time speaking slot.[34]

In the general election campaign, perhaps in response to Reagan's attempt at moderation on race or out of desperation at the lowered enthusiasm for Carter in the black community, Carter made a rather pathetic attempt to link Reagan to the Ku Klux Klan. One of Carter's most prominent black supporters, Andrew Young, warned blacks that if Reagan got elected it would be "okay to kill niggers." Carter also tried to draw attention to Reagan's support for white rule in Africa. These efforts largely backfired, as Reagan's careful balancing on race and his cheerful personage made these wilder claims about his alleged racism seem strained and desperate, at least to most whites.[35]

In Reagan's final campaign in 1984, he continued to lessen the role race played in his rhetoric. The "old" Reagan of 1976 made a brief appearance when he attacked busing in Charlotte, North Carolina, but the comment was so unpopular locally and nationally that it was never repeated. Polls showed that one of Reagan's few areas of vulnerability heading into the 1984 campaign was that he was perceived as unconcerned about justice and fairness, in part because of his stance on racial questions. However, rather than addressing these issues head-on, Reagan's campaign reinterpreted his tax reform proposal as a question of fairness. As Reagan's pollster put it, "rather than attempting to outdo Mondale on the fairness issue by more aggressively going after the black vote we took the tax issue and turned it into a fairness issue."[36]

In response to Reagan's first-term policies on race, the few black leaders who had supported him in 1980 were nowhere to be found in his reelection effort. The civil relationship he had initially with the NAACP vanished in angry charges and countercharges. Almost the only outreach Reagan's campaign had to black voters was a pathetic billboard campaign telling blacks that three black boxers (Muhammad Ali, Joe Frazier, and Floyd Patterson) were behind Reagan.

The anger in black America was so great that hundreds of thousands of blacks responded to voter registration drives led by Jesse Jackson and others in 1983–1984, which greatly frightened white Republicans in the South. The response of the Reagan campaign and affiliated groups was to exploit that fear to register whites. As one Reagan supporter attested, "Jesse Jackson made [white] people so mad . . . for every black vote he got, the Republicans and independents registered two whites."[37] Reagan's victory showed how polarized the nation was by the actor from California. At the very moment that white America (and to a lesser extent, Asian and Hispanic America) was crowning Reagan president by one of the greatest margins in American history, blacks were even more unanimously rejecting him.

From his first campaign speech in 1964 to his final appearances on the campaign trail in 1984, Reagan demonstrated a sustained lack of interest in wooing black votes or, perhaps more directly, a sincere interest in wooing the votes of whites who were opposed to or fearful of black progress. Of course, millions of Americans rallied to Reagan for nonracial reasons, and Reagan never practiced the kind of crude racist politics of Strom Thurmond in 1948 or George Wallace in 1968. Reagan always reacted to accusations of personal racism by challenging his accusers to show a single racist statement that he had ever made, and he often resorted either to the timeworn stories of his childhood opposition to racism or to dry recitations of the number of blacks appointed when he was governor of California. At one point, Reagan told a crowd of Republican blacks that he would have made more public references to his "record" number of black appointees, but he did not want to practice "cheap politics."[38] At the same time, Reagan had no aversion to occasionally using the cheapest of politics on the other side of the racial fence, such as exploiting white southern fear of a black vice president.

The twenty-year history of Reagan the campaigner shows a peculiar arc. While his debut speech in 1964 avoided race and racial issues, Reagan highlighted racial issues such as busing, affirmative action, and welfare when the backlash against black progress and black riots became white-hot from 1966 to 1972. Reagan had a lot less to say about race in 1980 and 1984. Perhaps this was simply because the public was less concerned about these issues, or because Reagan's reputation as a strong opponent of civil rights legislation was so well established that it was unnecessary to bring it up to reap electoral rewards. Yet Reagan's deft appeals to the Wallace bloc helped transform his party. Along with Richard Nixon's 1972 campaign, Reagan's 1968, 1976, and 1980 campaigns brought about a great electoral shift in the party coalitions, as millions of low-income and middle-class whites in the suburban North and American South trended Republican. While it would be false to attribute the entirety of that shift to race, along with national security, moral values, and crime, it was crucial to the change.

Campaigns cannot be studied in a vacuum, however. The promises made on the campaign trail often end up shaping the subsequent governing policies, and those policies in turn shape the next election.

Reagan on Racial Policies: Backlash on the Back Burner

Reagan's first elected office was the governorship of California from 1967 to 1975. In his two terms, he took credit for radically reducing California's welfare rolls, as well as cutting taxes. While he was never popular with California's black community, race was not central to his agenda. As opposed to governors in the South during the same period, Reagan did not have to address fundamental questions of black equality such as integration and intermarriage. During his tenure, California did not experience the massive urban unrest of the Watts riot of 1965. Nor did it face the highly symbolic issues of honoring Martin Luther King Jr. or the Confederate flag. Also, unlike more recent Republican governors around the country, Reagan did not make opposition to affirmative action and racial admissions policies at state universities central to his administration. On his election to the presidency, however, a whole array of racial issues required his attention. In almost every instance, Reagan took positions that either exacerbated tensions with the black community or failed to ameliorate the existing ones.

Reagan's economic policies were widely perceived, accurately or not, as responsible for the brief but deep recession of 1982–1983. Many black leaders argued that Reaganomics itself was racist. It certainly affected blacks more seriously than it did whites, although this could be said of every recession, given the stubborn gap between white and black unemployment. Still, as Stephen Carter points out, at one point during Reagan's first term, black unemployment was above black approval for Reagan.[39]

Reagan's administration consistently argued that blacks were not being well led, that their leadership was in part responsible for conveying an inaccurate picture of Reagan's attitude on race. Reagan actively sought to recruit and mentor a new generation of conservative black leaders, who could eventually supplant the existing black leadership. Ultimately, however, Reagan failed to make black conservatism anything more than a fringe movement in the black community.

Among the reasons for that failure was Reagan's consistent insensitivity to black concerns. In 1982, his administration suggested that tax exemptions should be granted to southern private academies that refused to admit blacks. While a very minor issue for Reagan and for most Americans, it was a high-profile concern for southern Republicans like Congressman Trent Lott, who wrote to Reagan demanding that segregated schools receive tax-exempt status. Private white southern academies had been the final segregationist response to the eventual victory of integration in the public schools, and for Lott and others, it was wrong to deny them tax exemption just because they discriminated. In fact, in a little-noticed portion of the Republican platform of 1980, this so-called unconstitutional vendetta against all-white Christian academies had been targeted for elimination. When the press got wind of the move, however, Reagan clumsily tried to claim that he had always supported the current policy and was merely hoping that Congress would enact the tax policy into law, rather than rely on the federal bureaucracy to deny the exemptions.[40] This patently false claim did nothing to stop the damage to Republican outreach to blacks. As Clarence Thomas, a leading black conservative, observed at the time, the effort to give tax exemptions to whites-only schools was the "death knell" for selling conservatism to blacks.[41] However, even in losing, some felt that Reagan had helped his standing among some whites: "Acting on its true instincts, the administration has lined up with suburban whites in opposition to government insistence on equal rights for minorities, thus signaling to white middle class Americans that their values and influence were once again predominant in national affairs."[42]

Every six months or so during Reagan's presidency, a racial issue would emerge that reminded black Americans where Reagan stood on race. As an opponent of the original 1965 VRA, Reagan's attitude toward the 1982 renewal of the legislation could have been predicted. While administration officials would not openly oppose renewal with a veto threat, they made it clear that they would not be unhappy to see the bill's opponents win, and they sought to weaken the VRA if possible.[43] The message that Reagan was reluctant to support even this nearly sacred part of the black agenda was devastating to his few black supporters. Similarly, Reagan actively sought out a confrontation with the Civil Rights Commission, another legacy of the civil rights era. He fired the controversial chair, Mary Frances Berry, as well as two other liberals, and sought to pack the panel with racial conservatives. Although the liberal commissioners ultimately won their seats back in court, the publicity hardly helped Reagan's racial image.[44]

Reagan's highest-profile engagement with race was the controversy over a holiday to honor Martin Luther King Jr. Reagan had long been ambivalent about King, as he had been about the entire civil rights movement. On the day King was shot, Reagan called the assassination "a great tragedy that began when we began compromising with law and order and people started choosing which laws they'd break."[45] The comparison between nonviolent marches and boycotts against racial discrimination and the assassination of a black leader was not likely to win Reagan many black supporters. Moreover, it echoed the criticisms of King's segregationist opponents since his earliest campaigns against racism. They argued that King, by challenging the status quo, was responsible for the violence that the white power structure used to defend its privileges. Reagan seemed to agree, just at the moment that King was entering the pantheon of martyred leaders. It was perhaps a historical irony that the long movement to honor King with a holiday would finally pass through Congress at a time when the man who had to sign the legislation was a lifelong opponent of government actions in defense of black civil rights.

Reagan faced pressure from his conservative supporters to veto the bill, which was opposed by such recovering racists as Senator Jesse Helms. Many conservatives believed that in addition to treasonably opposing the war in Vietnam, King had been a promiscuous philanderer and a communist. They pressed Reagan to release secret Federal Bureau of Investigation (FBI) files on King, despite the FBI's legal agreement with the King family not to do so. The fact that the FBI information had been gained through unconstitutional surveillance of a domestic political figure was inconsequential to Helms and his supporters. Reagan's true feelings in the matter can be gleaned from recently published correspondence. Writing to a hard-core right-winger who opposed the King holiday because of King's sexual immorality and left-wing tendencies, Reagan wrote, "I have the reservations you have but there the perception of too many people is based on an image not reality. Indeed to them the perception is reality. We hope some modifications might still take place in Congress."[46] Ultimately Reagan decided to sign the legislation, which might have done a little to help his image in the black community. However, asked about Helms's charges, Reagan gave credence to them, revealing his true attitude toward King. In one sentence, he lost whatever goodwill he might otherwise have generated.[47]

Reagan and his staff were well aware of the effect of these accumulated insensitive and offensive policies and missteps on the black community. Before a White House meeting with select black clergy, a staffer prepped Reagan for the reception he was likely to receive. After reviewing Reagan's attempts to weaken the VRA, undermine affirmative action, give tax exemptions to segregated schools, and cut urban spending, the memo concluded, "While no single category of acusation [sic] might in and of itself present a cause for alarm, the cumulative effect of all of them together has created distrust and bitterness within the minority community . . . there is a widespread sentiment that the Administration is 'anti-black' or engaged in a systematic effort to roll back civil rights achievements of the past."[48] Although this verdict was rendered midway through the first term, Reagan never launched any effort to change black America's opinion of him. Even in his appointments, Reagan showed greater interest in other minorities. While appointments of blacks to high government posts compared to the Carter years fell by more than 66 percent, Hispanic appointments held relatively steady.[49]

Perhaps the best that could be said of Reagan's racial policies as president was that he never put a high priority on any of them. One of the reasons for Reagan's success, particularly in his first term, was his relentless focus on three issues at the expense of all others: cutting taxes, raising defense spending, and confronting the Soviet threat. In particular, Reagan put almost all social policies on the back burner, and race was one of them. Indeed, one of his key southern supporters, Jerry Falwell, wrote to him in 1983 demanding action against racial busing.[50] While some items on Reagan's agenda, particularly weakening the VRA and taking strong action against affirmative action, were thwarted by Congress, in neither battle did Reagan commit much political capital.

When Reagan considered something truly vital, such as tax cuts or aid to the Nicaraguan contras, his lobbying and deal-making skills were considerable. No racial issue ever approached the core of Reagan's agenda. For Reagan, racial issues were most prominent on the campaign trail, not in office. The only possible exception was sanctions on South Africa. From the 1970s on, many Americans had been increasingly unhappy with the close association of the U.S. government with the racist government of South Africa. During Reagan's presidency, the movement to impose sanctions on South Africa grew to a crescendo. Facing considerable public and Congressional pressure to give in, Reagan fought long and hard for his policy of "constructive engagement" with the apartheid government. On no other racial issue of his presidency did Reagan exhibit such willingness to fight, even after it became clear that Congress had the votes to win on this issue. However, it is almost certain that what motivated Reagan here was not any love for the odious Botha government, but rather the belief that some South African commodities were vital to the U.S. military and, more important, that if the black majority took over South Africa, it would quickly become allied with the Soviet Union. What differentiated Reagan from many others who also saw the communist threat in southern Africa was that Reagan was so immune to the charge of racism by this point that he proceeded to pursue his policy goals regardless.

Reagan's Racial Legacy: Ironic and Subtle

Taken together, what did Ronald Reagan the man, the politician, and the president mean for race in America? What is Reagan's racial legacy?

First, and perhaps most important, Reagan contributed to the racial polarization of American party politics. In 1960, 32 percent of blacks voted for Richard Nixon. Since the Goldwater movement of 1964, black support for a Republican nominee has never risen above 13 percent. Reagan, as Goldwater's most prominent heir, continued and exacerbated the alienation of blacks from the Republican Party that began with Goldwater. He also was more responsible than any other Republican for the recruitment into the Republican coalition of racially conservative, former Wallace supporters. Ultimately, Reagan's success with such white voters, and his failure with blacks, had similar roots: his positions on sensitive racial questions. Reagan opposed every single civil rights act throughout the 1960s, when the vast majority of blacks could not vote or exercise most other basic civil rights. Even Goldwater had supported the Voting Rights Act, as a simple question of justice and fairness. Reagan even opposed a measure to give black American citizens the right to vote.

The legacy of Reagan's opposition to the Civil Rights Act and the Voting Rights Act—the foundational measures to give blacks basic equality —shaped his campaigns for his entire career. Modern black political, economic, and social equality, to the extent that it has been realized, has been built largely on the basis of these two legislative achievements. Those who opposed them at the time have either had to apologize and "repent," as Wallace and Senator Robert Byrd eventually did, or face a very difficult time with black audiences. Reagan never apologized for his earlier positions, although he tried to avoid discussing them as the Civil Rights Act and the Voting Rights Act in particular became nearly as sacred as constitutional amendments. But these indelible positions, while hurting Reagan among blacks, were a key factor in his early national appeal in 1968 and 1976 and, to a lesser extent, in his great victories of 1980 and 1984. More than any other political figure, Reagan was responsible for the defeat of the forces of civil rights within the Republican Party. In 1964–1965, Republicans were more positive toward civil rights for blacks than was the average Democrat. By the time of the Reagan revolution, while most Republicans, unlike Reagan, accepted the broad achievements and worth of the civil rights movement, the civil rights wing of the Republican Party was largely dead.

During his eight years in the Oval Office, Ronald Reagan never succeeded in reversing any of the major victories of the civil rights movement, as some of his most fervent supporters such as Falwell and Lott seemed to advocate. Reagan's presidency can be seen as an ironic affirmation of the triumph of black equality. A generation earlier, President Dwight Eisenhower ultimately institutionalized the New Deal by failing to overturn any of its core programs, even though Eisenhower and his supporters had opposed some of them for years. In the same way, part of Reagan's legacy is that the legislative victories of the civil rights movement and the moral stature of its great leader, Martin Luther King Jr., have become part of the fabric of American politics, unchallengeable for the foreseeable future. If even Ronald Reagan, who had opposed all the major civil rights acts and harbored grave doubts about Dr. King and the civil rights movement, was forced to sign the renewal of the VRA and a bill authorizing a holiday for King, no other president was likely to reverse the achievements of the civil rights era, even assuming such a person could be elected.

While Reagan did not leave much of a policy legacy on civil rights directly, his appointments to the judiciary have had and will continue to have a serious impact on race relations. Reagan appointed hundreds of federal judges who, like him, were either ambivalent about or hostile to the great achievements of the civil rights movement. In all the major cases trimming back Warren court decisions or affirmative action, Reagan appointees occupy a prominent position. A cursory look at *Adarand v. Pena* (affirmative action) or *Shaw v. Reno* (voting rights) shows that while Reagan never succeeded in ending affirmative action or weakening the Voting Rights Act directly, his appointees went a long way toward his stated goals.

In the end, Ronald Reagan's legacy was a missed opportunity for African-Americans. Had Reagan been less convinced of his own absolute immunity to any taint of racism, criticism of his policies by blacks might have led him to reach out to blacks and to offer them compromise positions on major racial issues. Reagan was without question the dominant force in his party from the fall of Nixon in 1974 to his departure from politics in 1989. Had Reagan met black Americans halfway on a few issues or paid more attention to the black community, most blacks would not have been left with only one choice in every election from Goldwater to Bush. Instead, they got a president who appointed almost no blacks to high office and who did not recognize his only black cabinet appointee in one of the rare moments that they actually met.[51] Unlike Hispanics in the current era, who are courted by both parties, blacks, in the face of Reagan's relentless insensitivity to their history, achievements, and leaders, were left to be demonized or at best ignored by one party and often taken for granted by the other.

The lost opportunity represented by Reagan may best be gleaned in examining the record of his true ideological and political heir, George W. Bush. No other Republican has been as consistent or successful in his open emulation of Reagan, so much so that a perceptive analyst recently titled a chapter-length study of Bush "Reagan's Boy."[52] Amid all the stylistic, political, and policy similarities, perhaps the greatest domestic difference is their approach to race. Bush, while gaining very few black votes in either 2000 or 2004, has much better relations with individual black leaders than Reagan ever did. From his earliest campaigns, Bush has tried to pitch himself as a "different kind of Republican" on race. While some critics question the sincerity of his views, even they would have to concede that the Bush tone and approach are significantly different from Reagan's, who in his campaigns often seemed content to win the election on the basis of white votes. Hypocrisy is the tribute that vice pays to virtue; even if we assume that Bush is merely mouthing warm platitudes on race that he does not believe in, at least he feels the need to mouth them more often and more convincingly than Reagan ever did. And there is compelling evidence that Bush is in fact different from Reagan in more than words. Bush was willing to compromise on affirmative action, not under pressure from Congress, as Reagan did, but because of pressure from blacks in his administration. Blacks have made remarkable breakthroughs during his presidency, including unprecedented appointments, albeit in areas far away from domestic policies. A black woman, Condoleezza Rice, is not only one of Bush's very closest advisers, but is credibly mentioned as his successor. Bush committed major resources to black outreach in 2000 (although not so much in 2004) and has tried to use his antigay positions and his faith-based initiative to win over religious blacks. Despite some success using black antipathy for gay rights to woo black votes, Bush remains alienated from most African-Americans in the mass public and unable to win their approval in the polls. Bush has begun the difficult labor of giving blacks two acceptable options in presidential elections, but much of the reason the task is so challenging is because of Reagan's racial legacy. The man from Dixon who believed that he was absolutely innocent of an iota of prejudice against blacks left behind a party that was almost incorrigibly white.

4

When Character Was King?

Ronald Reagan and the Issues of Ethics and Morality

Kyle Longley

In 2001, a former speechwriter for President Reagan, Peggy Noonan, wrote a book, *When Character Was King: A Story of Ronald Reagan*. She emphasized, *"He was a giant*. He was our giant, a giant of history; we know that now, and we wish we could put our arms around him and rock him to sleep." Reagan's strength, according to Noonan, was that "he had courage. He always tried to do what he thought was right. And when doing what was right demanded from him great effort or patience or tenacity, or made him the focus of unending attacks and criticism, he summoned from within the patience and the tenacity and the courage to face it all. . . . And when his great work was finished he left, and went peacefully home."[1]

Noonan's title underscores her argument and those of many conservative writers that Reagan was a man of "character," as defined by one dictionary as the "inherent complex of attributes that determine a person's moral and ethical actions and reactions."[2] Accordingly, he never let polls determine his positions, cared little about how history would portray him, and sustained a vision of America that brought about economic prosperity and the end of the Soviet Union. He stood in marked contrast to Bill Clinton in the character debate. Nevertheless, Reagan's supporters recognize the critiques of Reagan regarding character, and they often try to turn the weaknesses noted by Reagan's critics into strengths or at the least neutralize them.

Of course, there are some significant problems for people such as Noonan who try to either excuse or explain questionable character issues relating to Reagan. This chapter asks several questions relating to the character issue. First, it challenges the method of comparison. Instead of focusing on Clinton, whom Reagan never faced in an election, why not choose as the point of comparison Jimmy Carter, whom Reagan defeated in 1980? Second, it reviews a particular issue, abortion rights, to examine where Reagan stood on it. Did he really stand by his principles on this complex issue? Finally, it looks at the corruption that characterized the Reagan administration, many of the culprits closely associated with the president since his days as governor of California. It also covers in detail the very sticky issue of the Iran-contra affair in order to place Reagan's character under a microscope. The ultimate conclusion is that Reagan was, as his defenders argue, not Clinton, but he was hardly beyond reproach. In the end, he was a pragmatic politician with significant flaws, who often subordinated ideology and principles for politics.

Creating the Straw Man: Choosing the Character Comparison

In the discussion of Reagan's character, most conservatives juxtapose his activities against those of President Clinton. For more than a decade, conservatives vilified Clinton and his wife, Hillary Rodham Clinton. Clearly, the Clintons provided plenty of fodder on the character issue, including the Monica Lewinsky affair and the pardons handed out as Clinton left office. While the number of scandals in the Clinton administration, including the number of advisers indicted or investigated, was not that far different from the eight years of the Reagan administration, the chorus of denunciations from the right has been deafening and has slanted the debate.

Dinesh D'Souza provides a representative example of what conservatives have said about Clinton: "His character flaws and naked pursuit of power and self-aggrandizement have led to numerous scandals—Whitewater, Travelgate, Paula Jones, the use of the Lincoln Bedroom for campaign fund-raising—which have demeaned the presidency and demonstrated Clinton's unworthiness to be leader of a great country."[3] Others have been equally strong in their criticisms, all the while raising Reagan up as the anti-Clinton in the realm of morals and ethics and, by extension, as the virtuous Republican versus the immoral Democrat.

There is a significant problem with the point of comparison, primarily that Reagan never ran against Clinton. In fact, the better choice of contrast would be Jimmy Carter, Reagan's opponent in 1980. Carter, however, provides a significant challenge for conservatives in the character debate. An evangelical, born-again Christian with a long history of principled positions, Carter has a record of untarnished public service and enviable dedication to serving his fellow Americans and others in his postpresidency. It is relatively easy to hold up Reagan as the consummate man of character against Clinton. On the issue of morality and ethics, however, Carter makes most people, including Reagan, pale in comparison.

Ironically, Reagan's victory over Carter ushered in a significant political force in the conservative movement and in American political culture as a whole: the religious right, as represented initially by Jerry Falwell and the Moral Majority. Many conservatives voted for Reagan based on his position on issues of abortion and school choice, despite his lack of a stellar record of churchgoing, his being the first president who was a divorcé, and his mixed record on abortion as California governor. Reagan's record has created tensions for conservatives in their struggle to sustain the notion that conservative leaders have a monopoly on good character, since Carter is a devout southern Baptist who attended services religiously, served as a deacon, and regularly taught Sunday school at the First Baptist Church of Plains, Georgia, and the First Baptist Church of Washington. The Reverend Billy Graham writes, "Many leaders, I am afraid, place their religious and moral convictions in a separate compartment and do not think of the implications of their faith on their responsibilities. Jimmy Carter, however, was not like that." He adds that Carter is "a man of faith and sterling integrity" and "undoubtedly one of our most diligent Presidents, persistent and painstaking in his attention to his responsibilities."[4]

The Georgian's credentials as living the Christian faith he espoused only increased after he left office. He devoted significant time and energy to writing books such as *Living Faith* (1998) and *Sources of Faith: Meditations on Scripture for a Living Faith* (1999). He opens the former book with the statement that "religious faith has always been at the core of my existence," an important insight into his own self-perception.[5] The latter book is a compilation of fifty-two Sunday school lessons that he developed over the years. Carter's numerous books, which highlight his faith and its origins, have sold exceptionally well. They prove that conservatives, much to their chagrin, lack a monopoly on a personal relationship with Christ.

Carter's open pronouncement of faith, publicly as a leader and within his written works, creates a substantial problem for conservatives determined to retain the moral and ethical high ground related to religion and politics for their movement. Therefore, they have emphasized Reagan's religiousness, striving to justify his irregular church attendance, deprecating the lack of a significant paper trail relating to his religious beliefs, and using his public pronouncements as demonstrating the depth of his relationship with God. They reach conclusions such as that of Steven F. Hayward that "Ronald Reagan's deep religious faith has been overlooked because, in his typical modest way, Reagan kept it hidden in plain sight."[6]

The most pronounced of these works is Paul Kengor's *God and Ronald Reagan: A Spiritual Life* (2004). In his introduction, he stresses "Reagan was said to be private about his faith, not sharing it with those around him. To a significant extent, that was true. Yet, there it was an endless trail of religious remarks that coursed unmistakably through his papers and letters. Almost everywhere I seemed to look, there he was: the religious Reagan, motivated in every aspect of his life and career by his spiritual convictions."[7]

Seeking to prove his point, Kengor stresses the religious origins of Reagan's thoughts and speeches. To his credit, there are some, but he stretches his arguments about Reagan as opposed to Carter, whose public statements and actions constantly reaffirmed his Christian beliefs. Reagan's allusions to the "evil empire" or the "shining city" become prominent parts of Kengor's argument, but he largely ignores that these ideas are imbued in all Americans, regardless of religion. Even secular humanists have the belief in American exceptionalism and the concept of good versus evil instilled in them by the educational system, the media, and other socializing agencies. In many ways, Reagan was representative of generations of Americans, espousing the ideals of U.S. history and political culture in public presentations, but that does not mean that he had a deep-down, abiding, long-term faith like Carter's. Like many other conservative writers, Kengor tries hard to tie everything (speeches, stories, actions) to Reagan's religion in order to compensate for the lack of overt signs of it in his everyday life. Conservatives desperately want to further the perception that the greatest conservative president was morally and ethically superior to all challengers because of his religious foundations.

In many ways, the efforts to promote Reagan's religious life for contemporary political purposes demean the president. Like most Americans, Reagan had no special interest in studying theological questions, learning the scriptures in depth, or overtly proselytizing his faith. Yet he believed the basic concepts of the Christian faith, including prayer and divine intervention. In many ways, Reagan was the norm, compared to the exceptions like Carter and the pastor's son, Woodrow Wilson, whose deep abiding faith consistently guided their decisions. Ultimately, efforts by conservatives to prove such a faith in the case of Reagan are intellectually dishonest and disingenuous, driven by political motivations rather than the desire to fully understand the real nature of Reagan's religion.

However, Carter's actions, as well as his public statements and writings, must be seen in context in order to fully reveal the depth of his commitment. As a matter of character, Carter typically stood firm in his principles, which were rooted in his Christian faith. A representative example occurred even before Carter entered politics. In the mid-1950s, Carter reluctantly returned home to Plains, Georgia, from military service to take over the family business. He arrived at a time of great turmoil in the South, when the segregated system was under fire from the *Brown v. Board of Education* decision. White segregationists mobilized to disrupt attempts to end the old system of discrimination. One way was the creation of the Southern Citizens' Council, composed of the leading members of communities, including lawyers, businessmen, and doctors.

The segregationists needed unified efforts to hold the line. In Plains, the Southern Citizens' Council pressured Carter to join. With a strong belief in equal rights imbued in him through his religious beliefs, Carter refused. The group threatened to boycott his store, but he remained resolute. Several of his friends offered to pay his dues and allow him to remain in the shadows, but he steadfastly refused. A boycott followed that nearly ruined him, but he remained loyal to his principles and survived despite the economic loss. As he began his political career he avoided overt and covert uses of race, helping break a cycle of using race baiting for political advantage, a courageous stand during a difficult time in Georgia and the South.[8]

There are many other examples of Carter remaining loyal to his political principles and Christian beliefs. An important example was his emphasis on human rights as a cornerstone of American foreign relations when he took the presidency. He built on the idea of an early statement: "What we seek is . . . a foreign policy that reflects the decency and generosity and common sense of our own people."[9] Emphasizing human rights had a significant realist application regarding the Soviet Union as such an approach sought to change its behavior and to win the moral high ground in the struggle for the hearts and minds of the people of the nonindustrialized world. At the same time, Carter's approach rejected the short-term appeal of cooperating with dictators who trampled on the rights of people with a zeal equal to that of the communists. He heartily criticized South Africa for apartheid, denounced the Argentine military for its gross human rights abuses, and took actions to promote democracy and freedom around the globe.

Of course, there were problems with his choices. First, he was not always consistent in his application of policy focusing on human rights, a problem exacerbated by tensions in the foreign policy bureaucracy that undermined its application, especially conservatives in Congress and the military who believed that such a policy aided the communists against America's authoritarian allies. Carter consistently criticized the Soviet Union for its human rights abuses and retaliated in 1980 with the grain embargo and boycott of the Moscow Olympics, as well as significant military buildup, and he implemented his human rights policy in Latin America, but failed in uniform application in Iran and other areas. For this, he was bitterly chastised by conservatives, including prominent members of the Reagan administration such as Jeane Kirkpatrick, who argued that the United States could work with authoritarian, pro-American states but not totalitarian, pro-Soviet states. When Carter wavered, conservatives criticized him; when he was steadfast, they did the same. Like Reagan, Carter showed that principles were often subordinated to realpolitik. Still, many analysts note that the idea was correct even if the application failed.

Perhaps the most definitive and public way that Carter lived his principles and demonstrated his character was after he left the White House. While most presidents in the last half-century have retired from public life, occasionally emerging to accept large gifts for speaking engagements, Carter has done more for his fellow Americans and others in the world. Besides publishing more than fifteen books and giving thousands of speeches, he has lived his faith by working to provide housing for low-income people through Habitat for Humanity, and working to eradicate diseases such as river blindness and guinea worm disease, and to promote children's immunizations and mental health through the Carter Center.[10]

In addition, Carter has labored through the Carter Center to promote human rights and democracy around the world. He has worked as an election monitor and negotiator in Central America, the Middle East, the

Balkans, and Asia, trying to hammer out deals to stop the unending cycle of tension and violence. A good example occurred in 1994, when the Clinton administration faced off with the military dictators in Haiti over their coup against the democratically elected government of Jean-Bertrand Aristide. When negotiations failed and American troops prepared for an invasion that probably would have cost thousands of lives, Carter worked with Colin Powell and former Georgia senator Sam Nunn to remove the military junta and transfer power to Aristide. Despite strong opposition by some within the Clinton White House and Congress, Carter succeeded: the military leaders stepped down, preventing significant bloodshed in what has been termed the "immaculate invasion."[11]

Despite his efforts, critics from the left and right chastised Carter for his work with dictators and other sordid characters in his mission to establish peace and stability. Yet, as his proponents highlight, at least he tried to do something and in most cases achieved significant successes as a private diplomat. One writer observed, "Jesus, whom Carter worships, was said to have conducted his ministry among the downtrodden, among lepers and prostitutes. As a private citizen with no rank other than former President, Carter deals regularly with inhabitants of godforsaken villages and renegade leaders whom American officials ordinarily refuse to touch."[12]

Conservatives recognize the value of Carter to Democrats in the values issue, especially contrasting Reagan's lack of a humanitarian agenda during and after the presidency. As historian Douglas Brinkley highlights, "The self-serving pursuits of his extant predecessors appealed to Carter even less: Ronald Reagan had sold the cachet of his U.S. presidency to the Japanese for $2 million in speaking fees; Gerald Ford spent much of his time in Palm Springs working on his golf swing while collecting director's fees from corporate boards; and Richard Nixon was holed up in New Jersey with his Dictaphone in an endless quest to remake his image from dirty crook to international sage."[13]

As a result, conservatives have increasingly launched biting attacks on Carter to try to influence public opinion. A good example is Steven F. Hayward's *The Real Jimmy Carter: How Our Worst Ex-President Undermines American Foreign Policy, Coddles Dictators, and Created the Party of Clinton and Kerry*. This is a misleading title as Hayward focuses on Carter's postpresidency in only 30 of the 231 pages of the book. Ultimately, however, he concludes "not since Theodore Roosevelt has an ex-president been as peripatetic or troublesome to his successors as Jimmy Carter," adding that "every public figure deserves to have myths and inaccuracies debunked, but Jimmy Carter's failures are rooted in the character and ideology of the man himself."[14]

While denigrating Carter, supporters of Reagan blame his lack of activity since leaving the White House, other than writing his memoirs, testifying in several trials of former administration officials, and taking exorbitant speaking fees, on the onset of his Alzheimer's disease. However, neither before nor during his political career had Reagan shown any interest in special projects like Habitat for Humanity or the Carter Center. He retired, which was the norm rather than the exception, and that is fine, except when comparing his example to that of Carter, who increasingly set the standard for the behavior of ex-presidents.

Jimmy Carter's character, both in rhetoric and action, provides conservatives with significant challenges when trying to paint Reagan in a positive light. If they focus on Clinton, which they invariably do, they have a much easier task in making Reagan look good. However, when they juxtapose the two candidates who ran in 1980, the picture changes as Carter clearly shines as a result of writings, his personal record, and his long history of humanitarian efforts. Thus, if people want to focus on character and the presidency in contemporary America, the starting point should be Carter, although conservatives clearly understand the challenges that result.

A Matter of Conscience and Principle? The Abortion Issue

While points of comparison are significant, the true test of character in politics remains the commitment of a person to an unpopular position and subsequent action without fear of the consequences. Reagan's supporters, especially evangelical Christians, focus on his opposition to abortion as demonstrating this character. Peggy Noonan emphasizes, "taxes, SDI, and abortion were issues that captured his imagination" as "he could *see* the fetus kicking away from the needle."[15] Noonan, as well as others, liked to quote a section from Reagan's famous "evil empire" speech that "human life legislation ending this tragedy [abortion] will someday pass the Congress, and you and I must never rest until it does."[16] D'Souza underscores that Reagan's "greatest regret was that he was unable to do more as president to protect the lives of the unborn and that America would never be 'completely civilized' as long as abortion on demand was legal."[17] Each year, pro-lifers dedicate their rallies to Reagan and constantly use his quotes to further their political agenda.

While Reagan may have believed in the horror of abortion, there was a significant gap between rhetoric and practice that undermines efforts on his behalf to substantiate that he never paid attention to polls in his decisions. A few of the inconsistencies regarding abortion include his signing into law one of the country's most liberal abortion laws as governor of California, his appointment of two pro-choice Supreme Court justices, his failure to publicly embrace the pro-life movement for fear of alienating pro-choice Republican voters, and the noticeable absence of a postpresidency effort to support the pro-life movement. The record suggests that some of his advisers, more than Reagan, were willing to take on the contentious topic and that competing visions in the administration caused inaction, ultimately leaving an extremely ambivalent legacy.

One of the dark stains on his pro-life record occurred early in Reagan's political career. When Reagan became California governor, state law allowed for legal abortions only to save the life of the mother. In 1967 legislators, including many prominent Republicans, introduced a therapeutic abortion bill, which permitted legal abortions in the case of rape and incest and threats to the mother's physical and mental health.[18]

Reagan's handling of the issue reflected divisions in his family and his staff. Advisers Lyn Nofziger and Edwin Meese supported the bill, while Bill Clark opposed it. Reagan met secretly with Cardinal Francis McIntyre (which he initially denied doing), who firmly agreed with the argument of the Catholic bishop of Sacramento that "the unborn child, however brief its existence, is clearly identified by science even in embryonic form as belonging to the human family." On the other hand, Reagan's influential father-in-law, physician Royal Davis, backed the liberalization. Reagan would admit later "I have never done more study on any one thing than on the abortion bill."[19]

While Reagan personally agonized over the decision on the bill, his office issued an immediate statement promising that he would sign the legislation, which won victory in the California Assembly in June 1967. He did and Therapeutic Abortion Act went into effect. As opponents predicted, ideas effectively communicated to Governor Reagan, abortions skyrocketed from 518 legal abortions in 1967 to more than 199,089 in 1980 when Reagan took over as president, the total number exceeding 1,444,778 in that period in California alone.

Furthermore, during his next six years as governor of California, Reagan did little to try to overturn the statute, merely holding the ground against extending its provisions to fetuses with perceived deformities.

His attention turned to other priorities, including tax cuts and law and order issues. In turn, California (as in many cases) set a trend for the liberalization of abortion policies at the state level, a process culminating in the 1973 Supreme Court decision *Roe v. Wade,* which made legal abortion the law of the land.[20]

Even his most strident supporters such as D'Souza acknowledge that Governor Reagan's actions relating to abortion were a colossal failure. However, they argue that this disappointment made him more committed to stopping abortion as president, although the exact timing of the conversion that was not calculated to win conservative support is unclear. For example, in the period from 1975, when he left the governorship, until he took over as president, Reagan wrote 1,044 pieces, most for radio speeches. Of those, only one focused extensively on the abortion issue.[21]

Supporters would respond that once Reagan focused on national politics, his interest in abortion intensified. In July 1979, he spoke in favor of a constitutional amendment allowing the procedure only if a threat to the mother's life existed.[22] He also backed Congressman Henry Hyde's efforts to restrict federal funding for abortions, a position also supported by Democrats including President Jimmy Carter and Congressman Al Gore of Tennessee.[23] The presidential primary saw him paint George H.W. Bush as pro-choice, and during the regular campaign, his rhetoric brought northeastern and midwestern Catholics and southern evangelicals into the Republican fold, helping ensure a decisive defeat of Carter.

Once in office, Reagan supported the efforts of Senators Orin Hatch and Jesse Helms to push constitutional amendments severely weakening abortion rights. Yet the most important and long-lasting action of Reagan regarding abortion rights was his appointment in 1981 of Sandra Day O'Connor to the Supreme Court. Rather than backing the conservative choices such as Antonin Scalia and Robert Bork, Reagan followed up on his campaign promise to appoint a woman to the highest court. This was done despite the virulent opposition of Moral Majority head Jerry Falwell, who called on all "good Christians" to oppose the appointment, and the National Right to Life Committee, which highlighted O'Connor's record as a member of the Arizona Senate when she promoted a family planning bill that overturned one that banned abortions.[24]

Despite such criticisms, Reagan defended his nomination of O'Connor, telling one constituent who denounced his selection that "I am confident I made the right decision" and that "I feel as deeply as you do about the issue of abortion."[25] In his memoirs, he emphasized that "the only litmus test I wanted, I said, was the assurance of a judge's honesty and judicial integrity" and that "I appointed her and she turned out to be everything I hoped for."[26]

If the abortion issue was central to his view of the nomination process, then it played virtually no role in the choice to nominate O'Connor. This decision had a long-term and significant impact on the abortion debate in America. For more than twenty years, O'Connor consistently voted with the majority to uphold the basic principles of *Roe v. Wade* as well as other liberal interpretations of family planning outside of the abortion debate. Over and over again, O'Connor remained a swing vote in the abortion debate, leaving some pro-life critics disillusioned with the early statement that Reagan made in regard to their issue.

Nevertheless, Reagan's supporters would respond that the president followed this mistake with efforts to correct the problem. In 1986, he nominated Antonin Scalia to the Supreme Court receiving unanimous Senate approval. Scalia has been an ardent opponent of abortion, although whether this was the litmus test for Reagan as much as Scalia's strict constructionist interpretation of the Constitution remains unclear. Certainly, people in the administration and the Justice Department liked his position on abortion, but the president's true position remains murky because of the ambiguity of his first choice and the absence of any discussion in his memoirs.[27]

Then, in 1987, Reagan sought to appoint another justice, Robert Bork, who had solid credentials as an opponent of abortion (at least wanting to return it to state jurisdiction), but had been passed over three times for nomination, once by Ford and twice by Reagan. Again, whether the choice hinged on Bork's overall judicial and political record on abortion remains unclear as several people stressed that Reagan did not have much of a personal connection to the nominee. Although urged by many people to avoid the controversy, especially in the wake of the Iran-contra scandal and the return of Democrats to the control of the Senate in 1986, Reagan sent the nomination forward.

The nomination process was arguably the most bitter in American history. Civil rights groups, abortion rights organizations, and civil liberties groups all lined up against Bork, citing his long history of opposition to much of what the Court had done during the Earl Warren and Warren Burger years, including *Roe v. Wade.* In hearings, Bork promised to support the precedents established and several senators extracted concessions regarding the First and Fourteenth Amendments as well as abortion and discrimination, but his efforts failed to win approval. The Senate voted 58–42 to reject the nomination, with many Republicans joining the opposition to create the most lopsided defeat in history.[28]

Reagan's actions during the whole process were limited. In mid-August, as the debate heated up, the president left for a twenty-four-day vacation at his California ranch. During that time, he made few public statements and no efforts to lobby for the nominee. In fact, his first phone call to senators did not come until September 30, long after most senators had decided their vote. Despite urging by some advisers, Reagan also failed to even try to reach out to conservative southern Democrats who could possibly have been persuaded to support Bork.[29] The president appeared distant during the process and unwilling to expend much political capital in defense of Bork, despite protestations by some of his aides, including Attorney General Ed Meese, that he did work for the nomination.[30]

The embarrassing nomination of Douglas Ginsburg followed. Ultimately, he withdrew after the conservatives found out that his wife, an obstetrician, had performed abortions. More important, he revealed that he had smoked marijuana as a young man. Into his place stepped Anthony Kennedy, who won confirmation. While he had never publicly expressed his views on abortion, his Catholicism heartened social conservatives, who hoped that he would take his seat and work to overturn *Roe v. Wade.*

In the long term, they were disappointed. Kennedy voted to restrict the procedures, but consistently backed upholding the 1973 decision. The final result was that Reagan's appointments, rather than overturning *Roe v. Wade,* sustained it into the twenty-first century. His first appointment, Sandra Day O'Connor, clearly was pivotal and failed the litmus test regarding abortion, a point underscored by her opponents. The Scalia appointment was a victory, although it is unclear that he supported overturning *Roe v. Wade* or returning jurisdiction to the states (many of which would have sustained the decision).[31] Finally, Kennedy's appointment helped protect the basic concepts of *Roe v. Wade.* Clearly, Reagan's record on the Supreme Court was mixed and never matched the rhetoric, as abortion never appeared as a litmus test.

Besides the Supreme Court nominees, there are other examples of ambivalence in Reagan's abortion record. He and his allies slashed funding to domestic and international family planning services. Also, speechwriters led by Justice Department lawyer Michael Uhlmann penned an article for

Reagan in *Human Life Review* that further explained his pro-life position, a piece that ultimately became a booklet, *Abortion and the Conscience of the Nation* (1984). He previewed an antiabortion film in the White House and hosted private events for antiabortion leaders.

Despite such actions, Reagan and his advisers always maintained a distance from antiabortion groups. An important symbolic act, albeit one with substance, was that when Reagan received invitations from pro-life groups to speak at annual rallies in the nation's capital, he would make a telephone call rather than personally addressing the groups so that "he would not be seen with the leaders of the movement on the evening news." Lou Cannon notes that many of Reagan's supporters blamed this move on Michael Deaver and his fear of the negative images, but that Reagan "continued the practice after Deaver had left the White House."[32] It fit well with what a White House aide argued: "We want to keep the Moral Majority types so close to us they can't move their arms."[33]

There were other examples of the president's willingness to distance himself from the abortion controversy, especially as his presidency unraveled under the pressure of the Iran-contra affair and his closest advisers, including Nancy Reagan, became more prominent. She expressed happiness about Pat Buchanan's departure from the White House and the arrival of a new speechwriter. When she saw a first draft of Reagan's 1987 State of the Union address, she announced, "The parts about abortion have got to come out."[34] By the end of Reagan's presidency, clearly abortion had faded from political priorities as the vice president, George H.W. Bush, whose record was decidedly more liberal than Reagan's on the matter, began to take center stage.

While there was ambivalence during his presidency, Reagan's position after 1989 allowed him to make clearer his support for the overturning of abortion without fear of political ramifications. Yet he did not, although supporters would speculate that his Alzheimer's disease limited his efforts. Still, he found time to travel overseas, often receiving substantial fees for speeches. It was another five years before the family announced that he was suffering from the disease. As when he signed the abortion law as governor of California, there was a substantial lack of talk or action on the issue of abortion.

As an example, in the 726 pages of his memoirs, *An American Life,* which appeared in 1990, Reagan devoted significant space to writing about taxes, the Cold War, arms control, and many other topics. In the index, however, there is not one reference to abortion. There are no grand statements about the horror of the practice and the need for change or apologies for not doing more while in office. This lack contrasts significantly with the emphasis on abortion in the memoir by Pat Buchanan, the president's former speechwriter, who included a list of issues for what he characterized as a second constitutional convention. At the top was "for purposes of this Constitution, the unborn child shall be considered a 'person' whose right to life shall not be abrogated without due process of law."[35]

There was a similar lack of discussion of the issue among Reagan's former advisers, although Nancy Reagan wrote in 1989, "I can't get past the feeling that abortion means taking a life. But in cases of incest, rape, or the mother's well-being, I accept it."[36] Reagan's most prominent advisers, including Deaver and Meese, did not discuss the issue in their books as it was always subordinated to topics like taxes, law and order, and anticommunism.

In the final analysis, William Pemberton correctly notes that Reagan "kept his Religious Right followers happy through rhetoric and symbolic gestures, rather than through effective action on their agenda."[37] Nonetheless, Donald Critchlow observes that "whatever ambivalence they might have felt at times during Reagan's administration, grassroots conservatives forgot past ambivalence on both their and the administration's part. Their view of history placed Reagan as bold defender of their cause. His presidency imparted inspiration to carry their battle into the next millennium with the knowledge that Heaven's gates awaited them as onward-marching soldiers for a better nation."[38]

Still, the final evaluation of Reagan's position on abortion must look beyond the rhetoric to the actions. The overall record reveals his failure to truly advance the cause of the antiabortion movement. This failure reflects ambivalence within the Republican Party as economic conservatives and social liberals (civil libertarians) such as Barry Goldwater clashed with social conservatives determined to impose their moral values on the country. These cleavages persisted within the administration and Reagan's own family. Ultimately, if character requires sacrificing for unpopular beliefs, Reagan clearly failed the test in this area, despite the refusal of social conservative Republicans to recognize the fact.

The Incorruptible President?

Reading many of the biographies and works on Reagan by conservatives, leaves the impression that the former president was a man of scrupulous character, especially when contrasted with Clinton. In many ways, Reagan's supporters appear to place their president on an equal footing with George Washington and his "I cannot tell a lie" myth. However, under closer scrutiny, Reagan's record fails to correspond with those perceptions. He often told lies, in private and public, confusing stories he read or movie plots with real events. In addition, a disproportionate number of officials in his administration, including many close to the president, perpetrated acts that were at the least unethical and often criminal. Finally, questions raised by the president's performance during the Iran-contra affair significantly undermine his supporters' perception of a man of scrupulous character. In the end, Reagan was a politician whose unethical actions may have paled when compared to Clinton's, but they were hardly those of a role model.

One of the areas that requires closer scrutiny is Reagan's truthfulness. Lou Cannon emphasizes, "Reagan long ago learned to accept as the truth whatever version of events he used to explain things. This habit served him well politically but has proved a barrier to historical reconstruction."[39] Even Reagan's supporters, such as D'Souza, acknowledged the problem: "Even the careful scrutiny of White House aides could not prevent him from reciting an incident he had read about somewhere but didn't verify, or the news item that he remembered with one or two embellishments." D'Souza adds in an excuse for the president: "Reagan was unapologetic, because to him the stories were 'morality tales,' and the particular incident at hand was only an illustration of a broader theme. As he saw it, just because this or that particular detail might be erroneous did not mean that the moral of the story was invalid."[40]

There were many examples of this problem. An often repeated story that Reagan liked to tell (including once to the Congressional Medal of Honor Society in 1983) was that of a B-17 pilot in a damaged plane who refused to bail out because one of the gunners was too badly hurt to eject: "He took the boy's hand and said, 'Never mind, son, we'll ride it down together.' Congressional Medal of Honor, posthumously awarded." There were several problems with the story, including how people would know about the conversation if the two crewmembers died. A reporter investigated the claim, comparing it to the stories of the 434 Medal of Honor winners in World War II, and found no matching evidence. Ultimately, observers concluded that Reagan took the story from either a movie, *A Wing and a Prayer,* or a *Reader's Digest* story. While White House spokesman Larry Speakes argued "if you tell the same story five times, it's true," the issue of Reagan's truthfulness remained.[41]

In another case, Reagan told two different people that during World War II he had been in the Signal Corps and filmed the horrors of the Holocaust firsthand when U.S. troops liberated the death camps. Reagan told this story to Israeli prime minister Yitzhak Shamir, emphasizing "from then on, I was concerned for the Jewish people." He later repeated the account to Simon Wiesenthal, emphasizing that he had shown the films to people who questioned the extent of the Holocaust. The White House tried a variety of tactics to disengage from the story. James Baker emphasized that Reagan acknowledged that he had never left the country during the war and that he never said anything to the contrary. The White House also tried to argue that Shamir and Wiesenthal lacked the English skills to properly understand the president. This was a poor effort to cover up since both men had more than satisfactory English skills not to have confused the same story told at different times.[42] Ultimately, the furor died down and the press moved onto other stories.

Reagan's penchant for not telling the truth in such situations rarely backfired on him as he rarely admitted the absence of truth and many people, including journalists covering the president, either did not have the curiosity to check the facts or merely attributed them to the president's age or way of doing things. For Reagan, the act of apologizing for lying would have been like submitting a retraction in a newspaper, one that people rarely read; the original statement had the most effect. However, it pointed to moral ambiguity that no matter the origin highlighted a consistent problem faced by his aides in keeping the president grounded in reality and the fact-checkers from highlighting that what the president said (or wrote, for that matter) was the truth. While Regan's defenders may defend his lack of truthfulness, they have held their opponents, such as Bill Clinton and Al Gore, to different ethical standards than Reagan when they skewered them about similar exaggerations or distortions.

Another substantial problem involving the moral and ethical dimensions of Reagan's character lies in the corruption that plagued his administration. While the president does not appear personally involved in the scandals (except for Iran-contra), his lack of interest in the events unfolding and his defense of close associates involved in various public and private scandals established a tone of corruption to it. This created a serious blot on his record and character as a serious culture of corruption existed in his administration.

At least 138 officials from the Reagan administration were convicted, indicted, or investigated for criminal actions, the most of any president's administration through that time (other reports place the number at 190).[43] One of the most damaging cases involved Secretary of Housing and Urban Development Samuel R. Pierce Jr. and many employees, who were implicated in influence peddling and theft involving millions of dollars. During the investigations, a congressional subcommittee sought the testimony of Pierce, who became the first cabinet member since Albert Fall in the Teapot Dome scandal to invoke the Fifth Amendment.[44]

Ultimately, even the administration's staunchest supporters condemned the scandal. James J. Kilpatrick wrote, "It now appears that the taxpayers will take a loss of at least $2 billion on a cozy little, sleazy little, greedy little deals that were made." He went on: "Let it be said up top: the primary responsibility for this debacle lies squarely in the lap of Ronald Reagan. The buck stopped there. For the eight years of his administration, it now seems evident, the president paid virtually no attention to this huge costly department."[45] When combined with the savings and loan crisis, the Pierce scandal cost taxpayers a significant price tag for the gross corruption that plagued both programs.

Closer to the president, scandals plagued people who acted as Reagan's longtime senior aides and chief advisers. There had always been suspicions about many of the people around the president and how they enriched themselves through their connections to him. Several, like John Poindexter, had difficulties winning congressional approval because of allegations of misconduct even before entering the White House.

The first to receive punishment for his actions was Michael Deaver, who left the White House in 1986. An investigation of his lobbying activities after leaving the White House found that he had committed perjury. He received a three-year suspended sentence and was ordered to pay a $100,000 fine and perform community service.[46] Soon after, a jury found Lyn Nofziger guilty of three violations of the Ethics in Government Act, which was passed in 1978 in response to Watergate and several other scandals. He received a fine of $30,000 and ninety days in jail. An appeals court overturned the conviction, but the damage had been done to his reputation and, by extension, to his boss.[47]

By far, the most serious charges arose against Reagan's longtime close associate Attorney General Edwin Meese. Numerous charges of impropriety evolved, leading to seven-and-a-half-years of investigation for failing to report travel reimbursements, violation of conflict-of-interest rules, filing of false income tax returns, and intervention on behalf of Wedtech to help the company secure defense contracts and an oil pipeline from Iraq to Jordan. In 1987, a special independent counsel began investigating charges of bribery, fraud, and other illegal activities.[48]

Attacks on Meese often came from partisan Republicans. Criticisms mounted from within the Justice Department, where morale plummeted under Meese's leadership. Graffiti appeared calling Meese a "crook" and a "pig." Terry Eastland, a former speechwriter and strongly conservative Republican in the Justice Department, emphasized that Meese "left his shirttail hanging out at such length that it was easy for those who wished him ill to try to pull him down."[49]

The most serious challenge arose from two partisan Republicans, Deputy Attorney General Arnold Burns and Assistant Attorney General William Weld (future governor of Massachusetts). In March 1988, they resigned in disgust and met with Reagan to explain their decision. In that meeting, Burns denounced the flagrant violations of conflict-of-interest rules, criticized Meese for shaming the "temple of justice," and told Reagan that the morale in the department was the lowest "probably since the founding of the republic." Weld concluded that if the decision were left to him, he would seek an indictment against the attorney general. Despite the protests, Reagan continued to support Meese until he finally resigned in August 1988.[50]

The investigation of Meese continued for more than a year afterward. The federal prosecutor, with the approval of U.S. Attorney Rudolph Giuliani, publicly called Meese "a sleaze."[51] The final report by special prosecutor James McKay in July 1988 concluded that Meese had "probably violated the criminal law" but declined to prosecute on the four matters because "there is no evidence that Mr. Meese acted from motivation for personal gain."[52] McKay added that it appeared that Meese had taken bribes but that there was "insufficient evidence" for an indictment.[53] While Meese declared vindication, the Justice Department's Office of Professional Responsibility issued a report in 1989 saying that Meese's conduct "should not be tolerated of any government employee, especially not the attorney general."[54]

Haynes Johnson notes that Reagan's defense of his colleagues was a sign of loyalty, but also that "it signaled something more serious about the ethical standard Ronald Reagan set as president of the United States. He never bothered to establish stricter standards of conduct. Nor did he ensure that existing ones were properly enforced. In eight years in office he never made a single formal address on the question of government ethics, never issued a single call for adherence to higher standards."[55] Another historian writes that Reagan's attitude resulted in a "record of ethical malpractice which, if it lacked the wholesale plundering of the public treasury experienced in the Grant and Harding administrations, surpassed even those years in the frequency with which Reagan appointees were obliged to resign (they were never fired) for illegal or unethical practices."[56] The problem lay partly in Reagan's style of rule and his tendency to ignore bad things, a pattern developed in response to his alcoholic father. In any event, the record of corruption within the administration was significant, a point underscored by the most disruptive element of the administration, the Iran-contra affair.

The Iran-contra affair creates great difficulties for Reagan's supporters. If they argue that he was a dynamic leader in control of U.S. foreign policy, then they must accept that he knew about the various levels of the lies and cover-up of the affair. If they argue that he had no knowledge of the affair, then he was not in command of the situation, which would weaken the idea that he really influenced anything in foreign relations.

The most common way that Reagan's supporters defend the entire affair is to dismiss it as a political witch-hunt. Peter Wallison argues that the Iran-contra matter was "at most, a foreign policy blunder" and merely "another example of the destructive tendency to criminalize political or policy disputes."[57] One of the convicted conspirators later pardoned for his actions, Elliott Abrams, agrees in his book *Undue Process: A Story of How Political Differences Are Turned Into Crimes.*[58] Other conservatives blame the affair on Reagan's personality; Peggy Noonan, for example, claims that "Reagan was a romantic, and this time paid dearly for it."[59]

The entire Iran-contra affair revolved around two issues that had perplexed the Reagan administration since it took over. The first was an international effort against terrorism and the other was the funding of the anti-Sandinista contras. In both cases, frustrations mounted from the inability to find easy solutions to complex problems, especially the contra issue, which engendered significant domestic opposition from those fearful of getting embroiled in another Vietnam and associating with people intimately tied to the dictatorship of Anastasio Somoza. These frustrations resulted in the near collapse of the Reagan administration and permanently stained its reputation.

The battle against international terrorism had intensified, especially during the 1970s after the killing of Israeli hostages at the 1972 Munich Olympics and the taking of the American hostages in Iran. From day one, President Reagan had declared, "Let terrorists be aware that . . . our policy will be one of swift and effective retribution."[60] Problems heightened early on when the Israelis intervened in southern Lebanon to stop border attacks by Islamic militants. In response, in 1982, President Reagan placed American troops in Beirut as "peacekeepers" who became allied with the Christian militia, angering Lebanese Muslims and Palestinian exiles. This resulted in the disastrous suicide bombing of a U.S. marine barracks that claimed the lives of 241 marines on October 23, 1983. Devastated, the United States began its withdrawal from Lebanon soon after, but with increased resentment toward those in the Middle East who had perpetrated the heinous act.

The problems became even more acute when terrorists and their allies, supported by Iran and Syria, began kidnapping prominent U.S. citizens (including CIA agent William Buckley) who remained throughout the region. The president, genuinely concerned about the human suffering of American citizens, soon became embroiled in a scheme to use the Iranians to win the freedom of the hostages in exchange for arms.

While the imbroglio in Lebanon and the Middle East was unfolding, the administration had devoted significant time and energy to trying to overthrow the Nicaraguan Sandinistas, who had taken control in 1978 following their successful revolution against the longtime U.S.-supported dictator Anastasio Somoza. Believing that the Sandinistas were stooges of Fidel Castro and by extension the Soviet Union in an area deemed vital to the United States, Reagan and many conservatives developed a near obsession with the anti-Sandinista contras, whom Reagan characterized as "freedom fighters" and the "moral equivalent of the Founding Fathers." However, many Americans looked on the contras as the remnants of the Somoza regime and worried about the United States being drawn into another Vietnam.[61]

The problems began for the administration in 1982 when Congress, a group characterized by Reagan as the meddlesome "committee of 535," began restricting contra aid in response to atrocities and lies being told by administration officials regarding U.S. assistance to the group. Boland I in 1982 and Boland II in 1984 severely restricted military aid to the organization, leading the president to support questionable efforts through private citizens and foreign groups to keep the contras together.

He instructed National Security Council (NSC) head Robert McFarlane in 1985 to keep the contras together "body and soul" and did not question a basic policy of outside groups, in this case the Saudis, providing assistance to circumvent the congressional edicts.[62] Soon, McFarlane put a marine lieutenant colonel in the NSC, Oliver North, in charge of the operation.

In June 1985, despite the behind-the-scenes move toward trading arms for hostages, Reagan told the press that "America will never make concessions to terrorists—to do so would only invite more terrorism. Once we head down that path, there would be no end to it."[63] In July 1985, in a speech to the American Bar Association, he called Iran part of a "confederation of terrorist states . . . a new international version of Murder Inc." Grouping the Iranians with North Korea, Cuba, Libya, and Nicaragua, he branded them as "outlaw states run by the strangest collections of misfits, Looney Tunes and squalid criminals since the advent of the Third Reich."[64] These public statements, combined with Reagan's open support of efforts such as Operation Staunch, which sought to limit Iran's access to military equipment, were the public face of the administration regarding the rogue nation.

Despite the public statements, the administration moved toward dealing with the Iranians in the summer of 1985. A shady, exiled Iranian arms dealer, Manucher Ghorbanifar, made overtures to the Israelis, who reached out to U.S. officials, especially McFarlane. The Iranian promised an opportunity to deal with Iranian moderates who could possibly be in a position to shape the country after the death of the Ayatollah Ruholla Mussaui Khomeini.

That summer, serious debates began within the administration about selling tube-launched, optically-tracked, wire-guided (TOW) missiles to Iranians in return for assistance in securing the release of American hostages in Lebanon. Secretary of Defense Caspar Weinberger vigorously opposed the deal, arguing that it was probably illegal. Nevertheless, on July 27, the president phoned McFarlane and told him, "I want to find a way to do this."[65] Less than two weeks later, there was a meeting in the private presidential quarters with Vice President George H.W. Bush, Secretary of State George Shultz, Weinberger, and McFarlane at which the president called for a "go slow" strategy that the opponents of the deal view as stopping it. However, a few days later, Reagan called McFarlane into his office and stated, "Well, I've thought about it . . . and I want to go ahead with it . . . I believe it's the right thing to do."[66]

Over the next four months, there would be a series of arms transfers to Iran through the Israelis. After the second one, captors in Lebanon released a hostage, Benjamin Weir. Additional layers developed as North incorporated outside people led by retired general Richard Secord, and John Poindexter replaced McFarlane. Problems resulted as the Iranians asked for more sophisticated weaponry and the arms-for-hostages nature of the operation became more apparent, even though the numbers of people released remained very small.[67] The administration labored to develop plans that circumvented congressional oversight, although Shultz and Weinberger continued to vigorously resist the scheme. The supporters settled on the direct transfer of arms to the Iranians. By January 17, 1986, Reagan signed a finding, the third one in six weeks, that approved the plan. He wrote in his diary, "I agreed to sell TOWs to Iran." There was no question about his knowledge of the plan.[68]

Over the next year, Secord and North set about their task with zeal. The sale of weapons produced a significant cash flow, not only for the American government but also for the Iranian middlemen who skimmed off significant amounts. North and Poindexter funneled the money into a Swiss bank account and began using it to fund contra operations in Central America. A couple of American hostages were released as expected, but the terrorists in Lebanon simply took more afterward.

Ultimately, the whole plan unraveled in October 1986 when the Sandinistas shot down a plane carrying supplies to the contras flown by an American pilot, Eugene Hasenfus. Not long after, a Lebanese magazine, *Al-Shiraa,* broke a story about the arms-for-hostages activities of McFarlane, which started a firestorm of follow-up news reports.

In response, Reagan went on national television on November 13, believing that he could convince the American people of the sincerity of his attempt to open a diplomatic door to Iran to counter Soviet efforts. He filled the speech with inaccuracies and outright lies, including the claim that all the spare parts "could easily fit into a single cargo plane" and that "we did not—repeat, did not—trade weapons or anything else for hostages, nor will we." Within a short period, pollsters began producing their findings. In one, only 14 percent of the American people believed the president's version of the story.[69]

Reagan followed the performance with a nationally televised press conference on November 19. Working off a flawed chronology of events prepared by Poindexter, the president again misled the American people. When queried about Israel's role in the arms exchange, Reagan responded, "We, as I say have had nothing to do with other countries or their shipments of arms or doing what they're doing." When asked whether terrorists had learned from the entire episode that America would deal with them, Reagan responded, "I don't see where the kidnappers . . . gained anything. They didn't gain anything. They let the hostages go." He went on to blame the media for breaking the story and preventing more hostages from being released. When a *Washington Times* reporter asked why Reagan would not admit the mistake and move on, Reagan retorted, "I don't think a mistake was made. It was a high-risk gamble, and it was a gamble that, . . . I believe the circumstances warranted."[70]

Several investigations of the administration began soon after. Poindexter and North vigorously shredded important evidence, and Poindexter and CIA director William Casey lied to the House and Senate Intelligence Committee, saying that no one in the government knew about the arms deal and that they believed that the shipments were oil-drilling equipment. At the same time, the administration began damage control. On November 25, Reagan announced the resignation of Poindexter and the firing of North, whom only a short while afterward Reagan called and told "Ollie, you're a national hero."[71] The day after, Reagan agreed to the formation of a special review board headed by John Tower, former senator from Texas. Then on December 2, Reagan asked for a special independent counsel to investigate the affair, including the diversion of funds to the contras. Within a couple of weeks, Lawrence Walsh received the appointment and began his investigation.[72]

Over the next year, the different groups set about their tasks of investigating the entire arms-for-hostages scheme and diversion of funds to the contras. Reagan's performance in talking with the Tower Commission was especially troubling. On January 26, 1987, Reagan, to the great astonishment of several of his advisers, including White House counsel Peter Wallison, admitted to approving the first shipment of arms by the Israelis and agreeing to subsequent resupply of weapons to the Israelis. Reagan essentially supported McFarlane's timeline given to the Senate Foreign Relations Committee a few days earlier.[73]

During a follow-up interview, Wallison and Vice President Bush helped Reagan develop a different timeline, emphasizing that Reagan was surprised to learn of the shipment of arms, thus supporting the testimony given by his chief of staff Donald Regan. During this interview, Reagan asked Wallison for the memorandum that (Wallison) had prepared. Then, Reagan read it verbatim to the committee: "If the question comes up at the Tower Board meeting, you might want to say that you were surprised." A flabbergasted committee stopped the interview at that point. An exasperated member of the committee, Edmund Muskie, expressed frustration that the president consistently asked about the hostages and obviously agonized "over this thing every day, and yet he can't remember anything about it. My God!"[74]

Reagan's final statement on the issue came a little while afterward. He wrote a memo explaining that he had no notes or records to help him with his memory of the approval of arms sales in August 1985. "My answer therefore and the simple truth is, 'I don't remember, period.'"[75]

Reagan's testimony to the Tower Commission sparked much controversy and skepticism. It appeared to establish a pattern that reminded some people of Reagan's appearance before a federal grand jury twenty-five years earlier. When he was president of the Screen Actor's Guild, his close friend Lew Wasserman (who had been his agent and had helped him delay his entry into the reserves) and the Music Corporation of America (MCA) received a very favorable contract from the guild that departed significantly from typical guild rules. Charges of conflict of interest and benefits accruing to Reagan plagued him for several years in Hollywood and the contract eventually sparked a Justice Department investigation.[76]

When called to testify in 1962, Reagan defended his actions, arguing that he had done what he believed was best for the actors despite the appearances of impropriety. When pressured by the prosecutor on a pivotal part of the contract, Reagan responded, "I don't recall it, no . . . I don't honestly recall." He then added that during the summer of 1952, when these events occurred, he was in Glacier National Park making a movie and "so it's very possible there were some things going on that I would participate in." In reality, the movie he noted was not filmed until the summer of 1954. Yet the "I do not remember defense" worked, and while the incident tarnished his reputation, it failed to be a lethal blow to his political aspirations.[77]

While the arms-for-hostages portion of the crisis was significant, the potentially more damaging charge originated from the decision to divert to the contras the funds from the sales of the arms. This charge led many administration insiders to fear a possible impeachment. Reagan consistently denied the charges and the death of Casey provided some cover, as he would have most likely been the one who provided direct information on the subject to the president. Still, Brent Scowcroft, who served on the Tower Commission and remained a partisan Republican, believed that Reagan may have been told about the diversion of funds, but that he forgot or more likely that someone like Poindexter "may have found a way in briefing him to say, 'By the way, we've found a way to help the contras from this too.' It may have been done in a casual way that didn't raise the legalities of the issue."[78]

There remained a great deal of skepticism about the extent of Reagan's knowledge of the diversion. His active role in soliciting funding from outside groups, including the Saudis and Taiwanese as well as private Americans, and claims that he actively involved himself in such matters raised suspicions of what he knew and when. Reagan political adviser Stuart Spencer emphasized, "the key to the whole thing is he can remember. There are some things he remembers very poorly, but I think he wants to remember them very poorly. He really has a good memory."[79] Oliver North wrote after the affair "the president didn't always know what he knew."[80]

The Tower Commission report, released in late February 1987, concluded, "The arms transfers to Iran and the activities of the NSC staff in support of the contras are case studies in the perils of policy pursued outside the constraints of orderly process." It added, "The Iran initiative ran directly counter to the administration's own policies on terrorism, the Iran/Iraq war, and the military support to Iran. The inconsistency was never resolved. . . . The result taken as a whole was a U.S. policy that worked against itself."[81]

On March 4, 1987, Reagan went on national television and told the American people, "A few months ago I told the American people I did not trade arms for hostages. My heart and my best intentions still tell me that's true, but the facts and the evidence tell me it is not."[82] While he would continue to deny the truth in his memoirs, he had been persuaded by his new chief of staff, Howard Baker, and others of the need to accept some responsibility. The backhanded acknowledgment, nevertheless, deflected much of the criticism, as even the normally critical *Washington Post* acknowledged that "President Reagan gave the right speech last night . . . he admitted plenty, and he pledged to redeem the damage in his final two years in office."[83]

The investigations continued in the House and Senate and through the special prosecutor, Lawrence Walsh. The congressional committees concluded that the responsibility for the entire affair lay with Reagan, noting, "If the President did not know what his National Security Advisers were doing, he should have."[84]

The Walsh investigation lasted several years and led to the conviction of thirteen of Reagan's subordinates, including Poindexter, Weinberger, North, and Abrams. North and Poindexter had their convictions overturned on technicalities and several people received pretrial pardons from by then President George H.W. Bush, but others served time and Reagan had to testify in several of the trials.

Regarding Reagan, the Walsh Report, released in 1994, argued that Reagan's actions "fell well short of criminality which could be successfully prosecuted" and that no information existed that could prove without a doubt that he "knew of the underlying facts of Iran/Contra that were criminal or that he made criminal misrepresentations regarding them." Instead, Walsh argued that "President Reagan created the conditions which made possible the crimes committed by others by his secret deviations from announced national policy as to Iran and hostages and by his own determination to keep the contras together 'body and soul' despite a statutory ban on contra aid." In conclusion, Walsh underscored that he had uncovered facts that at the least should have given Congress pause and that impeachment should have been discussed.[85]

Other critics, including many who had served in the White House with Reagan, began writing their memoirs in the aftermath of the Reagan presidency. George Shultz emphasized that "the U.S. government had violated its own policies on antiterrorism and against arms sales to Iran, was buying our own citizens' freedom in a manner that would only encourage the taking of others, was working through disreputable international go-betweens, was circumventing our constitutional system of governance, was misleading the American people—all in the guise of furthering some purported regional political transformation, or to obtain in actuality a hostage release." He went on to blame McFarlane, Poindexter, and Casey for selling his version "to a president all too ready to accept it, given his humanitarian urge to free American hostages."[86]

Part of the problem with the Iran-contra affair may have been the administrative style of Reagan. Martin Anderson emphasized that Reagan "made decisions like an ancient king or a Turkish pasha, passively letting his subjects serve him, selecting only those morsels of public policy that were especially tasty. Rarely did he ask searching questions and demand to know why someone had or had not done something. He just sat back in a supremely calm, relaxed manner and waited until important things were brought to him."[87]

Whatever the final outcome in relation to Reagan, the Iran-contra scandal reflected poorly on his leadership style and integrity. If supporters continue to insist that the president had no knowledge of the arms-for-hostages transfer or diversion of funds, then Reagan had limited influence on the implementation of U.S. foreign policy at a critical juncture of his presidency. If this was the case, then he had little control over successes attributed to him in relation to the Soviet Union or elsewhere. On the other hand, if he was a vibrant president, then it was likely that operations related to the Iran-contra affair were within his purview and that he committed numerous criminal violations such as perjury. Most likely, the truth was somewhere in between, with Reagan clearly understanding the arms-for-hostages exchange but having only vague ties to the diversion. In this case, he clearly lied to the American people on his role and most likely to investigators with the Tower Commission, but failed to rise to criminal behavior for the diversion of funds. The latter scenario clearly demonstrates that he would lie to protect himself when pressed, hiding under the guise of memory lapses. This scenario severely damages any characterization of him as the role model for character.

In the final analysis, while conservatives try to portray Reagan as a paragon of virtue, the lies, the corruption, and the scandals that surrounded him were significant. While not rising to the levels of Richard Nixon, they closely parallel those of Bill Clinton and other administrations such as Grant's and Harding's in degree and frequency. Reagan's propensity for exaggeration and lies, whether in his stories or his role in Iran-contra, further undermines the arguments of Noonan and others. In the end, Reagan was a politician in a profession in which the truth factor often escapes even the most ethical of people. While more honest and forthright than many others, Reagan failed to reach the standard of the mythology of his followers and in many ways failed to rise to the standards established by his role models including Franklin Roosevelt.

Conclusion

As conservatives seek to enshrine Reagan in the pantheon of American leaders, other issues of character relating to Reagan call out for investigation. These include his personal life, which raises the issues that he was the only divorced American president, that his children often served as poster children for the dysfunctional family, and that his devotion to his second wife, Nancy, led to a reliance on an astrologer in his daily activities.

In another realm, there are the issues that arose after his presidency, when, during the short period that he remained active before the onset of Alzheimer's, he received million-dollar speaking engagements from the Japanese, spent time in court defending his former aides, and took huge gifts to refurbish his California ranch, some critics arguing that the money was payback for services rendered while in office (the gifts were claimed to be loans, but ones at very beneficial rates). In both cases, there are open areas for investigation that fit well into the issues of character that have been a cornerstone of the conservative movements' efforts to discredit Clinton and the Democrats and conservatives raise their stature in public debates over Reagan's character.

The final conclusion is that Reagan was not corrupt like many of the people surrounding him. On the other hand, he was not the glowing paradigm of character that Noonan and others seek to portray. His principles were flexible when necessary on issues such as abortion. He told lies when it suited his political purposes, and the Iran-contra scandal highlighted his lapses in judgment. When compared to Carter's, his moral and ethical positions fare much worse than when compared to Clinton's. Like most people, and especially politicians, Reagan failed the litmus tests of character on numerous occasions, but there were also successes that conservatives correctly highlight while ignoring those examples that fail to support their arguments. More research and debate should remain a cornerstone of the discussion of Reagan's legacy and how it applies to contemporary political issues relating to character.

The issue of Reagan's character, and in particular the mythology surrounding it, also fit nicely into the efforts of conservatives today to frame their candidate, George W. Bush, on the character issue. From the start, Bush wrapped himself in the Christian flag and accompanying moral and ethical standards. His work on his father's campaign in 1988 as liaison to the Christian Coalition imprinted on him the value of the evangelicals. When he ran for president, the efforts to win the character battle accelerated, aided in part by Clinton's misadventures and Gore's missteps on the topic of campaign finances and misrepresentations of his role in the creation of the Internet.

As Bush's presidency unfolded in the aftermath of September 11 and the run for reelection in 2004, a plethora of books started to appear extolling the virtues of President Bush as a man of principle and foresight. These include books such as David Frum's *The Right Man: An Inside Account of the Bush White House* (2003), Ronald Kessler's *A*

Matter of Character (2004), Karen Hughes's *George W. Bush: Portrait of a Leader* (2005), and Fred Barnes's *Rebel-in-Chief: How George W. Bush Is Redefining the Conservative Movement and Transforming America* (2006). In each, Reagan remains the standard that Bush has met or surpassed; like his predecessor, Bush appears above reproach on issues of corruption and ethical and moral dilemmas. Bush has remained steadfast in his visions of a strong America, even when those positions appear unpopular. To these authors and other conservatives, Bush is the right man at the right time with the character to lead the country and in some ways transform America.

There are also a significant number of books focusing on Bush's faith as the source of the ethical and moral decisions of his presidency, including a volume of his speeches, *George W. Bush on God and Country: The President Speaks Out About Faith, Principle, and Patriotism,* which appeared during the run-up to the 2004 election. Others include Stephen Mansfield's, *The Faith of George W. Bush* (2003), David Aikman's *A Man of Faith: The Spiritual Journey of George W. Bush* (2004), Paul Kengor's *God and George W. Bush: A Spiritual Life* (2004), and Joseph J. Martos's *May God Bless America: George W. Bush and Biblical Morality* (2004). These books focus primarily on the president's ethical and moral beliefs and how they evolved and are lived out through his Christian faith. While Kengor already has a track record in writings about Reagan and his Christian principles, most of these authors go far beyond merely tying Bush to his Christian values, largely because, unlike Reagan, Bush publicly makes statements and leaves a significant paper trail on the issue. Still, as with Reagan, evangelicals and conservative Christians have flocked to Bush's side and been a strong foundation of his political power.

There are also many within the president's inner circle who have promoted his straight forwardness and character. Condoleezza Rice argues that the most similar thing between Reagan and Bush is an assertion of moral certainty: "Many people are much more comfortable with on-the-one-hand-on-the-other-hand-explanations. But there are very often cases where there are not arguments on both sides. And I think President Bush has been pretty willing, when that is the case, to speak in black-and-white terms."[88]

Through 2005, the character issue remained a very positive rating for the president even when his poll numbers in many other areas began plummeting. However, in the wake of revelations about the lead-up to war in Iraq, the disclosure of the identity of Valerie Plame, an ousted undercover CIA agent, and the political scandals of the Republican Party, the polls numbers have eroded very quickly on even this strength. Only time will tell whether Bush will rebound in all areas, for once the damage is done, it is often difficult to overcome. Still, Bush supporters can take hope from Reagan's success after Iran-contra. George W. Bush could achieve the same, depending on how events unfold and his approach and attitude.

Epilogue

Contemporary Politics and
the Myths of Reagan

In January 2003, Bill Keller wrote in the *New York Times* an article about George W. Bush titled "Reagan's Son." He observed that "the party faithful have been pining for a new Reagan since Reagan, and for Bush the analogy has the added virtue of providing an alternative political lineage; he's not Daddy's Boy, he's Reagan Jr." Keller added that "Bush is not, as Reagan was, an original, but he has adapted Reagan's ideas to new times, and found some new language in which to market them." Even old Reagan supporters like Michael Deaver emphasized, "I think he's the most Reagan-like politician we have seen, certainly in the White House. I mean, his father was supposed to be the third term of the Reagan presidency—but then he wasn't. This guy is."[1]

As each preceding chapter in this volume has noted, the effort by the administration of George W. Bush to utilize the Reagan legacy has been significant. It began even before the presidential race started with the purchase of a ranch in 1999 where Bush could demonstrate his ties to the common people by being photographed cutting brush and driving around in a pickup truck. It continued with the campaign focus on "values," with Bush adopting the concept of the "compassionate conservative" and trying to take the hard edge off the traditional perceptions of conservatives, a task Reagan had performed well.

In many ways, Bush supporters, even those outside of the campaign, framed the comparison between Bush and Reagan early on. A *Wall Street Journal* reporter emphasized, "In the early weeks of this Bush administration, a veteran U.S. senator told me not to compare the new President to his father but rather to Ronald Reagan. The senator, who knew all three, said that while the first President Bush had been one of America's finest public servants, his son and Mr. Reagan had more greatness in them. Both shared deeper convictions that they had a larger mission to fulfill. The terrorist attacks of September 11 provided George W. both confirmation and direction for that sense of calling." The journalist acknowledged, "The current Bush administration has relished comparisons to the Gipper. Like Mr. Reagan, . . . George W. would confound his critics with historic accomplishments because, like Mr. Reagan, he possessed a fervor about America and its transformative nature."[2]

There are many other similarities underscored by analysts. As one observer noted, "Reagan asked Americans to dream heroic dreams, but he rarely asked them to give up anything. President Bush, even with a war on, shows no greater desire to bet on sacrifice." In the area of abortion rights, Reagan "was always treated by the anti-abortion constituency as a kindred spirit. This is another Reagan lesson Bush seems to have taken on board: if you have underlying credibility with the advocacy groups, you do not have to undertake quixotic efforts on their behalf."[3]

Some of the comparisons were not always positive. As one analyst observed, "righteous purpose is strong stuff, and it can be highly flammable" as in the case of the Iran-contra affair. "Bush has not only rehired several of the Iran-contra intriguers, but has also reproduced elements of the climate in which the plot was hatched—obsessive secrecy, a premium on loyalty, a taste for working through foreign proxies, an impatience with Congressional oversight."[4]

The efforts to tie Bush to Reagan only increased after the latter's death in the summer of 2004. Journalist Howard Fineman wrote, after Reagan's death and before the Republican National Convention that would become a tribute to the Gipper, that "there is little risk, and a bit to gain, for Bush in associating with the Reagan aura. Voters on the left who think the comparison is damning to Bush weren't going to support him anyway; voters on the right who think the comparison makes Bush look small are going to vote for Bush anyway. Voters in the middle who still aren't sure what to make of Bush may see a wee bit more vision in his thinking—and vision is a thing every president (and every president running for re-election) needs."[5]

In the long run, significant problems have evolved for Reagan supporters and the efforts of the Bush people to tie Bush to the former president. Bush's polls plummeted in the aftermath of the war in Iraq, the response to Hurricane Katrina, uncontrolled spending and deficits, and internal spying on Americans. In response, Reagan loyalists have increased their calls to focus on Reagan in his own light, not within the prism of the conservative movement of the twenty-first century and, in particular, George W. Bush.

The process had already begun even before Bush's decline in popularity, being led in part by Ron Reagan Jr. When the Bush team tried to exploit his father's death for its own political gain, Reagan counterattacked. An opening salvo occurred at his father's funeral in June 2004. "Dad was also a deeply, unabashedly religious man," he told the crowd and national television audience. "But he never made the fatal mistake of so many politicians wearing his faith on his sleeve to gain political advantage. True, after he was shot and nearly killed early in his presidency, he came to believe that God had spared him in order that he might do good. But he accepted that as a responsibility, not a mandate. And there is a profound difference."[6]

In an earlier interview in 2003, Reagan had stressed, "Some of the current policies are an extension of the '80s. But the overall thrust of this administration is not my father's—these people are overly reaching, overly aggressive, overly secretive, and just plain corrupt. I don't trust these people." He had taken a swipe earlier in 2000 at the GOP convention when he told a reporter that "the big elephant sitting in the corner is that George W. Bush is simply unqualified for the job. . . . What's his accomplishment? That he's no longer an obnoxious drunk?" He stressed his father's credentials in politics as union leader, governor, and candidate. "Sure, he wasn't a technocrat like Clinton. But my father was a man—that's the difference between him and Bush. To paraphrase Jack Palance, my father crapped bigger ones than George Bush." He added that his father "didn't have to ask Dick Cheney what he thought."[7]

The attacks continued after the Republican convention in 2004 when the Bush people made sure that Ronald Reagan received a central stage in the politics of memory. In a scathing article in *Esquire,* Ron Reagan talked about how Bush's attempt to exploit President Reagan's funeral and other efforts had backfired. "People were treated to a side-by-side comparison—Ronald W. Reagan versus George W. Bush—and it's no surprise who suffered for it." After a scathing rebuke to Bush for having "come to embody dishonesty itself," Ron Reagan concluded, "I'll acknowledge occasional annoyance at the pretense that he's somehow a clone of my father, but far from threatening, I see this more as silly and pathetic. My father, acting roles excepted, never pretended to be anyone but himself. His Republican party, furthermore, seems a far cry from the current model with its cringing obeisance to the religious Right and kill-anything-that-moves attack instincts."[8]

While Bush supporters dismiss the younger Reagan as jealous, a tool of the liberal media, or just seeking attention, increasingly hard-line ideological conservatives have begun attacking the president. Early attacks came from William F. Buckley and Pat Buchanan. In the latter's book, *Where the Right Went Wrong: How Neoconservatives Subverted the Reagan Revolution and Hijacked the Bush Presidency,* the former Reagan speechwriter denounced the "Bush doctrine" and the policy of preemptive war, which he described as "a prescription for permanent war for permanent peace, though wars are the death of republics." In particular, he attacked the invasion of Iraq, which was "our own Lebanon of 24 million Iraqis" and characterized by a guerrilla war where "U.S. prestige has plummeted." Buchanan argued that free trade, illegal immigration, and activist courts have undermined America, but saved his harshest critique for the party in power, concluding that "conservatism, as taught by twentieth-century leaders like Robert Taft, Barry Goldwater, Ronald Reagan, and Jesse Helms, is dead" and that there is "no conservative party left in Washington."[9]

Conservative columnist Jonah Goldberg asked different questions than Buchanan or the younger Reagan and focused on Bush's move away from traditional conservative economic viewpoints in a speech in January 2004. He highlighted a few quick facts, noting that George W. Bush has "increased federal spending on education by 60.8 percent; increased federal spending on labor by 56 percent; increased federal spending on the interior by 23.4 percent." Goldberg focused on the huge buildup of homeland security and chastises the president for signing a campaign finance bill, and other programs, stressing that he "signed the farm bill, which was a non-kosher piñata filled with enough pork to bend space and time; pushed through a Medicare plan which *starts* with a price tag of $400 billion but will—according to every expert who studies the issue—go up a gazillion-bajillion dollars over the next decade; . . . not vetoed a single spending—or any other bill, and he has no intention of eliminating a single department." Goldberg concluded with "read Tuesday's lead editorial in the *Wall Street Journal,* and you'll find that this is the spendiest (yes, that's right, 'spendiest') president in American history, second only to LBJ. Maybe there's something about presidents from Texas—they like everything big down there, including their government."[10]

Goldberg also made comparisons to other presidents who preceded Bush by emphasizing, "Ronald Reagan declared in his first inaugural that 'government is the problem.' George W. has never said anything of the sort. In fact, he even said last Labor Day, 'we have a responsibility that when somebody hurts, government has got to move.' The Gipper would have spontaneously burst into flames if he'd said something like that." He concluded, "Compassionate conservatism always struck me as the Republican version of Clintonism, rather than the Republican alternative to it."[11]

Others have joined Goldberg on the right, many concerned about large deficits and government expansion as well as issues such as the assault on civil liberties in the Patriot Act and domestic spying. New examples include Bruce Bartlett in *Impostor: How George W. Bush Bankrupted America and Betrayed the Reagan Legacy* (2006), which bitterly denounced Bush's policies. Like other writers, Bartlett seeks to defend Reagan's legacy by dismissing the ties between Bush and Reagan. With Bush's numbers spiraling downward and the effects of his economic and foreign policies becoming apparent, the frequency of attacks from conservatives will most likely increase.

On the other hand, ultimately, the Bush loyalists may take umbrage at those like Grover Norquist, who emphasized "Bush 43 is exactly where Reagan was, but he stands on Reagan's shoulders."[12] Bush, already having desperately sought to escape any shadow of his father, will probably seek to distance himself from comparisons over time as he attempts to define his own legacy. As he told NBC anchor Tom Brokaw in 2004, "[I] think of myself as a 'George W. Republican.'"[13]

Whatever the outcome of these battles, the issue of Reagan's legacy is not likely to diminish in importance for many years. A fuller picture should develop over time with the release of new primary documents, and debates inside and outside of the conservative wing of the Republican Party will help determine how Reagan and George W. Bush coexist. In the long term, a picture may develop of a contrast like that between Franklin Roosevelt and Harry Truman. Whatever the path, the debates over the Reagan legacy and its application to modern politics will continue well into the twenty-first century.

Notes

Introduction

1. *Arizona Republic,* February 17, 1999.
2. *New York Times,* October 21, 2003; *Christian Science Monitor,* November 7, 2001.
3. *Washington Post,* June 17, 2001.
4. Michael Kammen, *Mystic Chords of Memory: The Transformation of Tradition in American Culture* (New York: Knopf, 1991); David Waldstreicher, *In the Midst of Perpetual Fetes: The Making of American Nationalism, 1776–1820* (Chapel Hill: University of North Carolina Press, 1997). Liberals often do the same with John Kennedy since no strong, vibrant president has emerged since Franklin Roosevelt to represent their vision of America. That is why when *George* magazine did a story titled "Who Will Make Us Proud Again?" in August 2000, the editors selected two different covers. On one was John Kennedy and on the other Ronald Reagan.
5. Byron C. Hulsey, *Everett Dirksen and His Presidents: How a Senate Giant Shaped American Politics* (Lawrence: University Press of Kansas, 2000), 78.
6. Thomas A. Bailey and David M. Kennedy, *The American Pageant: A History of the Republic,* 8th ed. (Lexington, MA: D.C. Heath, 1987), 868.
7. As cited in Michael Schaller, *Reckoning with Reagan: America and Its President in the 1980s* (New York: Oxford University Press, 1992), 41.
8. *Arizona Republic,* June 6, 2001.
9. *Arizona Republic,* June 6, 2001.
10. Dinesh D'Souza, *Ronald Reagan: How an Ordinary Man Became an Extraordinary Leader* (New York: Free Press, 1997), 258.
11. D'Souza, *Ronald Reagan,* 23.
12. Historian Kristin Hass comments, "I think a lot of their impulse is born out of anxiety about how Reagan is going to be remembered. They must feel in order to hold on to the idea he was the greatest, they have to make it in stone everywhere." *Washington Post,* June 17, 2001.
13. *Wall Street Journal,* June 7, 2004.
14. *Abilene Reporter-News,* March 12, 2006.
15. *Washington Post,* June 17, 2001.
16. Memorable Quotes from *The Man Who Shot Liberty Valance,* IMDb, www.imdb.com/title/tt0056217/quotes.

Chapter 1

1. Multiple tributes to Reagan appeared in the *New York Times,* June 10–12, 2004; William E. Pemberton, *Exit with Honor: The Life and Presidency of Ronald Reagan* (Armonk, NY: M.E. Sharpe, 1997), 154; Peter Schweizer, *Victory: The Reagan Administration's Secret Strategy That Hastened the Collapse of the Soviet Union* (New York: Atlantic Monthly Press, 1994) and *Reagan's War: The Epic Story of His Forty-Year Struggle and Final Triumph over Communism* (New York: Doubleday, 2002), 280–285; Ann H. Coulter, *Slander: Liberal Lies About the American Right* (New York: Crown, 2002) and *Treason: Liberal Treachery from the Cold War to the War on Terrorism* (New York: Crown, 2003), 190; for more nuanced conservative analysis of Reagan's diplomatic achievements, see George P. Shultz, *Turmoil and Triumph: My Years as Secretary of State* (New York: Scribner, 1993) and John L. Gaddis, *The United States and the End of the Cold War* (New York: Oxford University Press, 1992); for an insightful analysis by the leading Soviet expert in Reagan's National Security Council from 1983 to 1987, see Jack F. Matlock, *Reagan and Gorbachev: How the Cold War Ended* (New York: Random House, 2004). Ronald Reagan's ghostwritten memoir of his presidency, *An American Life* (New York: Pocket Books, 1990), says little of substance on foreign policy.

2. Kiron Skinner, Annelise Anderson, and Martin Anderson, eds., *Reagan, In His Own Hand: The Writings of Ronald Reagan That Reveal His Revolutionary Vision for America* (New York: Free Press, 2001), 121, 60; Ronald Reagan, *Public Papers of the Presidents of the United States: Ronald Reagan, 1981–1989,* 8 vols. (Washington, DC: Government Printing Office, 1982–1989), 57. As of 2004, relatively little primary documentation exists for Reagan's foreign policy. The most extensive and reliable studies of Reagan-era foreign policy include Raymond L. Garthoff, *The Great Transition: American-Soviet Relations and the End of the Cold War* (Washington, DC: Brookings Institution Press, 1994), and Don Oberdorfer, *From the Cold War to a New Era: The United States and the Soviet Union, 1983–1991* (Baltimore: Johns Hopkins University Press, 1998). See also Beth A. Fischer, *The Reagan Reversal: Foreign Policy and the End of the Cold War* (Columbia: University of Missouri Press, 1997), and Matlock, *Reagan and Gorbachev.*

3. *New York Times,* October 20, 1980; *Public Papers, Reagan, 1983,* 262–264.

4. *Public Papers, Reagan, 1982,* 744–747; Robert M. Gates, *From the Shadows: The Ultimate Insider's Story of Five Presidents and How They Won the Cold War* (New York: Simon and Schuster, 1996), 194.

5. Carter, of course, not Reagan, had negotiated the hostage release during his final days in office. For months, Reagan and his aides feared the incumbent might pull an "October surprise" and spring the hostages as an election ploy. See Gary Sick, *All Fall Down: America's Fateful Encounter with Iran* (New York: I.B. Tauris, 1985).

6. *Public Papers, Reagan, 1981,* 57. Unlike conservative critics of détente, many career diplomats and academic experts believed that the strategy had, indeed, undermined the Soviet system by exposing its population to the outside world. On this point, see Garthoff, *Great Transition,* and Jack F. Matlock, *Autopsy on an Empire: The American Ambassador's Account of the Collapse of the Soviet Union* (New York: Random House, 1995). See also Matlock, *Reagan and Gorbachev.*

7. This point is stressed by Gates, *From the Shadows,* and by Schweizer in both *Victory* and *Reagan's War.*

8. Alexander Haig, *Caveat: Realism, Reagan, and Foreign Policy* (New York: Macmillan, 1984), 85.

9. Jane Mayer and Doyle McManus, *Landslide: The Unmaking of the President, 1984–1988* (Boston: Houghton Mifflin, 1988), 28, 52, 98–99.

10. James A. Baker, *The Politics of Diplomacy: Revolution, War and Peace, 1989–1992* (New York: G.P. Putnam, 1995), 26–27; Colin L. Powell and Joseph E. Persico, *My American Journey* (New York: Random House, 1995), 334.

11. Martin Anderson, *Revolution* (Stanford, CA: Hoover Institution Press, 1988), 289–291; John Updike, *Rabbit at Rest* (New York: Knopf, 1990).

12. Shultz, *Turmoil and Triumph;* Robert C. McFarlane and Zofia Smardz, *Special Trust* (New York: Cadell and Davies, 1994).

13. Chester Patch, "Sticking to His Guns: Reagan and National Security," in *The Reagan Presidency: Pragmatic Conservatism and Its Legacies,* ed. W. Elliot Brownlee and Hugh Davis-Graham (Lawrence: University Press of Kansas, 2003), 85–112.

14. David Stockman, *The Triumph of Politics: How the Reagan Revolution Failed* (New York: Harper and Row, 1986), 105–110.

15. Margaret Thatcher, *The Downing Street Years* (New York: HarperCollins, 1993), 463.

16. Anderson, *Revolution,* 81–97; Robert Scheer, *With Enough Shovels: Reagan, Bush and Nuclear War* (New York: Random House, 1982).

17. The evolution and politics of SDI are discussed in three excellent books. See Frances Fitzgerald, *Way Out There in the Blue: Reagan, Star Wars, and the End of the Cold War* (New York: Simon and Schuster, 2000); William Broad, *Teller's War: The Top Secret Story Behind the Star Wars Deception* (New York: Simon and Schuster, 1992); Michael Rogin, *Ronald Reagan, The Movie: And Other Episodes in Political Demonology* (Berkeley: University of California Press, 1987).

18. *Public Papers, Reagan, 1983,* March 23, 1983; Fitzgerald, *Way Out There,* 255–254; Pemberton, *Exit with Honor,* 131–132.

19. Gates, *From the Shadows,* 263–266.

20. Gates, *From the Shadows,* 263–266; Rowny and McFarlane are quoted in Oral History Conference, Brown University, May 7–10, 1998, cited in Beth Fischer, "Reagan and the Soviets: Winning the Cold War," in Brownlee and Davis-Graham, *Reagan Presidency,* 113–132; Matlock, *Reagan and Gorbachev.*

21. Reagan, *American Life,* 237–238; Schweizer, *Victory,* 20–21, 102–106, 205–215; Gates, *From the Shadows,* 200–225.

22. Skinner et al., *Reagan, In His Own Hand,* 12, 63.

23. McFarlane and MacEachin both cited in Fischer, "Reagan and the Soviets"; see also Pemberton, *Exit with Honor,* 153–154.

24. Shultz's memo of January 19, 1983, is cited in Fischer, "Reagan and the Soviets"; Matlock's views are detailed in his memoir cited earlier, *Autopsy on an Empire,* as well as in his *Reagan and Gorbachev.*

25. On the Soviet economy, see Richard Crockett, *The Fifty-Year War: The United States and the Soviet Union in World Politics, 1941–1991* (New York: Routledge, 1995), 210–213; Shultz, *Turmoil and Triumph,* 124; Pemberton, *Exit with Honor,* 154–155.

26. Schweizer, *Victory,* 24–32, 81–82, 202–205, 219–220, 236–243.

27. Martin Mayer, *The Greatest Ever Bank Robbery: The Collapse of the Savings and Loan Industry* (New York: Scribner, 1990).

28. Martin and Susan Tolchin, *Buying into America: How Foreign Money Is Changing the Face of Our Nation* (New York: Crown, 1988); Clyde Prestowitz, *Trading Places: How We Allowed Japan to Take the Lead* (New York: Basic Books, 1988).

29. Secretary of State Shultz persuaded Reagan to drop support for these thugs by warning that if they were forcefully toppled, they might be replaced by communist regimes. See Shultz, *Turmoil and Triumph,* 608–638. See also Raymond Bonner, *Waltzing with a Dictator: The Marcoses and the Making of American Philippine Policy* (New York: Crown, 1987).

30. Haig, *Caveat,* 101–105; *Public Papers, Reagan, 1981,* 57; Gates, *From the Shadows,* 200–225, 239–241, 354–356; Garthoff, *Great Transition,* 92–95. Most career CIA and State Department analysts believed that the Soviets were not behind the attack because the Kremlin saw the pope as a restraining force on anti-Soviet groups in Poland. However, some people, including members of the Italian parliament, continue to blame Moscow for the attack.

31. David C. Martin and John Walcott, *Best Laid Plans: The Inside Story of America's War Against Terrorism* (New York: HarperCollins, 1988).

32. Gates, *From the Shadows,* 177–178.

33. Gates, *From the Shadows,* 218–219; Michael Deaver and Mickey Herskowitz, *Behind the Scenes* (New York: William Morrow, 1987).

34. Michael Schaller, *Reckoning with Reagan: America and Its President in the 1980s* (New York: Oxford University Press, 1992), 152; *Public Papers, Reagan, 1982,* 581–585. The so-called Reagan doctrine is discussed in National Security Directives #32 (March 1982), #66 (November 1982), and #75 (January 1983). Reagan declared it national policy to oppose Soviet domination of Poland and Eastern Europe and to challenge Soviet initiatives in the third world. See Schweizer, *Victory,* 130–133; McFarlane, *Special Trust,* 219–222; Christopher Simpson, *National Security Directives of the Reagan and Bush Administrations: The Declassified History of U.S. Political and Military Policy, 1981–1991* (Boulder, CO: Westview Press, 1995).

35. Reagan, *An American Life,* 448–458; and Shultz, *Turmoil and Triumph,* 323–345.

36. Reagan news conference, *New York Times,* April 10, 1986.

37. Shultz, *Turmoil and Triumph,* 677.

38. Shultz, *Turmoil and Triumph,* 677–688.

39. Gates, *From the Shadows,* 251–252, 348–350. Two especially insightful studies of U.S. involvement in Afghanistan are Steve Coll, *Ghost Wars: The Secret History of the CIA, Afghanistan, and Bin Laden, from the Soviet Invasion to September 10, 2001* (New York: Penguin, 2004), and George Crile, *Charlie Wilson's War: The Extraordinary Story of the Largest Covert Operation in History* (New York: Grove Press, 2003).

40. Reagan Address to Nation, *New York Times,* March 17, 1986.

41. Mayer and McManus, *Landslide,* 71, 85–88.

42. David Fromkin and James Chace, "Vietnam: The Retrospect: What Are the Lessons of Vietnam?" *Foreign Affairs* (Spring 1965).

43. For the background of events in El Salvador, see Raymond Bonner, *Weakness and Deceit: U.S. Policy in El Salvador* (New York: Crown, 1984); Mark Danner, *Massacre at El Mozote: A Parable of the Cold War* (New York: Vintage, 1994).

44. Mayer and McManus, *Landslide,* 85–88; Schaller, *Reckoning with Reagan,* 152; Gates, *From the Shadows,* 242–249. Among the most reliable accounts of U.S. policy in Nicaragua and of the Iran-contra scandal are *Banana Diplomacy: The Making of American Policy in Nicaragua, 1981–87* (New York: Roy Gutman Touchstone Books, 1988); Theodore Draper, *A Very Thin Line: The Iran Contra Affairs* (New York: Hill and Wang, 1991). A sympathetic first-person account of Reagan's effort to placate critics of the Iran-contra debacle is presented by David Abshire, *Saving the Reagan Presidency* (College Station: Texas A&M Press, 2005).

45. *Public Papers, Reagan, 1985,* 228–229, 537; McFarlane, *Special Trust,* 68; Ben Bradlee, *Guts and Glory: The Rise and Fall of Oliver North* (New York: HarperCollins, 1988), 551.

46. John Dinges, *Our Man in Panama: The Shrewd Rise and Brutal Fall of Manuel Noriega* (New York: Random House, 1991).

47. Fred Greenstein, "Ronald Reagan: Another Hidden Hand Ike?" *Political Science and Politics* (March 1990): 7–13.

48. *Public Papers, Reagan, 1986,* 352–356.

49. Mayer and McManus, *Landslide,* 189–208.

50. Anatoly Dobrynin, *In Confidence: Moscow's Ambassador to America's Six Cold War Presidents, 1962–1986* (New York: Times Books, 1995), 484–485.

51. Reagan, *American Life,* 256–258, 269–273, 567, 580, 586; Oberdorfer, *From the Cold War,* 21.

52. Seymour M. Hersh, *The Target Is Destroyed: What Really Happened to Flight 007 and What America Knew About It* (New York: Vintage, 1987).

53. Oberdorfer, *From the Cold War,* 50–70.

54. Oberdorfer, *From the Cold War,* 70–74.

55. Garthoff, *Great Transition,* 167.

56. Oberdorfer, *From the Cold War,* 123–148; Garthoff, *Great Transition,* 220, 257–261, 520–221, 551, 554, 583, 592, 728, 767.

57. Matlock, *Autopsy on an Empire,* 121–123; Gartoff, *Great Transition,* 753–754, 759, 775.

58. Oberdorfer, *From the Cold War,* 189–209; Garthoff, *Great Transition,* 252, 283, 285–300, 524–525, 555, 593, 767; Matlock, *Reagan and Gorbachev.*

59. Oberdorfer, *From the Cold War,* 212–225.

60. Oberdorfer, *From the Cold War,* 263.

61. Oberdorfer, *From the Cold War,* 280.

62. Powell and Persico, *My American Journey,* 375.

63. John LeCarré, *The Secret Pilgrim* (New York: Knopf, 1991), 12.

Chapter 2

1. Alan Dundes, ed., *Sacred Narrative: Readings in the Theory of Myth* (Berkeley: University of California Press, 1984).

2. Peter Robinson, *How Reagan Changed My Life* (New York: Regan Books, 2003), 132, 242, 260; Dinesh D'Souza, *Ronald Reagan: How an Ordinary Man Became an Extraordinary Leader* (New York: Free Press, 1997), 29, 33, 264; Peggy Noonan, "Thanks from a Grateful Country," *Wall Street Journal,* June 7, 2004; William Kristol, "Reagan's Greatness: Giving a President His Due," *Weekly Standard,* November 10, 1997, 33–34; George Will, "His Greatest Role," *Wall Street Journal,* June 7, 2004; Charles Krauthammer, "Reagan as Optimist? Just a Liberal Slight," *Time,* June 14, 2004.

3. John W. Sloan, *The Reagan Effect: Economics and Presidential Leadership* (Lawrence: University Press of Kansas, 1999). The material on Reagan's economic policy making has been adapted from *The Reagan Effect: Economics and Presidential Leadership,* by John W. Sloan, copyright © 1999 by the University Press of Kansas, chapters 6 and 9. Used by permission of the publisher.

4. Lou Cannon, *President Reagan: The Role of a Lifetime* (New York: Simon and Schuster, 1991), 90–92.

5. Betty Glad, "Reagan's Midlife Crisis and the Turn to the Right," *Political Psychology* 10 (December 1983): 613.

6. Haynes Johnson, *Sleepwalking Through History: America in the Reagan Years* (New York: W.W. Norton, 1991), 67.

7. W. Elliot Brownlee and C. Eugene Steuerle, "Taxation," in *The Reagan Presidency: Pragmatic Conservatism and Its Legacies,* ed. W. Elliot Brownlee and Hugh Davis Graham (Lawrence: University Press of Kansas, 2003), 157.

8. Brownlee and Steuerle, "Taxation," 167–168.

9. Brownlee and Steuerle, "Taxation," 156.

10. Thomas Edsall, *The New Politics of Inequality* (New York: W.W. Norton, 1984), 210–211.

11. Brownlee and Steuerle, "Taxation," 156.

12. John F. Witte, *The Politics and Development of the Federal Income Tax* (Madison: University of Wisconsin Press, 1985), 232–233.

13. Brownlee and Steuerle, "Taxation," 159.

14. Brownlee and Steuerle, "Taxation," 158.

15. C. Eugene Steuerle, *The Tax Decade: How Taxes Came to Dominate the Public Agenda* (Washington, DC: Urban Institute Press, 1992), 50.

16. Steuerle, *Tax Decade,* 43.

17. Steuerle, *Tax Decade,* 58.

18. Brownlee and Steuerle, "Taxation," 163.

19. Brownlee and Steuerle, "Taxation," 168.

20. Brownlee and Steuerle, "Taxation," 167.

21. John F. Witte, "The 1986 Tax Reform: A New Era in Politics?" *American Politics Quarterly* 19 (October 1991): 445.

22. Michael J. Boskin, *Reagan and the Economy: The Success, Failures, and Unfinished Agenda* (San Francisco: Institute for Contemporary Studies, 1981), 158.

23. David E. Rosenbaum, "Senate, 74–23, Votes Tax Bill," *New York Times,* September 18, 1986. See also Ronald F. King, "Introduction: Tax Reform and American Politics," *American Politics Quarterly* 19 (October 1991): 417–425.

24. Witte, "1986 Tax Reform," 444.

25. Boskin, *Reagan and the Economy,* 122.

26. Witte, "1986 Tax Reform," 447.

27. Steuerle, *Tax Decade,* 121.

28. Jeffrey H. Birnbaum and Allan S. Murray, *Showdown at Gucci Gulch: Lawmakers, Lobbyists and the Unlikely Triumph of Tax Reform* (New York: Vintage, 1988), 286.

29. Birnbaum and Murray, *Showdown at Gucci Gulch,* 73. See also Timothy J. Conlan, Margaret T. Wrightson, and David R. Beam, *Taxing Choices* (Washington, DC: CQ Press, 1990), 71.

30. Albert S. Hunt, "Introduction," in Birnbaum and Murray, *Showdown at Gucci Gulch,* xiv.

31. Witte, "1986 Tax Reform," 443.

32. *Historical Tables,* Fiscal Year 1991 (Washington, DC: U.S. Government Printing Office, 1998), 21–22.

33. David Wessel and Gerald F. Seib, "How Reagan Recast Debate on Markets, Taxes—and Deficits," *Wall Street Journal,* June 7, 2004. See also Andrew E. Busch, *Ronald Reagan and the Politics of Freedom* (Lanham, MD: Rowman and Littlefield, 2001), 90.

34. Sidney Blumenthal, "Letter from Washington," *New Yorker,* July 19, 1983, 30.

35. Council of Economic Advisers, *Economic Report of the President, January 1982* (Washington, DC: U.S. Government Printing Office, 1982), 9–10.

36. John Herbers, "President Asserts Economic Policies Prove Effective," *New York Times,* October 14, 1982.

37. Mark Peffey and J.T. Williams, "Attributing Presidential Responsibility for National Economic Problems," *American Politics Quarterly* 13 (October 1985): 414.

38. Alonzo L. Hamby, *Liberalism and Its Challengers: From FDR to Bush,* 2d ed. (New York: Oxford University Press, 1992), 368.

39. Cannon, *President Reagan,* 275.

40. Martin Anderson, "The Reagan Revolution," *New York Times,* January 17, 1990. See also Robert L. Bartley, *The Seven Fat Years: And How to Do It Again* (New York: Free Press, 1992), 4, 6, 144.

41. Louis Uchitelle, "107 Months, and Counting," *New York Times,* January 30, 2000.

42. John Liscio, "A Presidential Report Card," *Barron's,* August 12, 1996, 30.

43. Council of Economic Advisers, *Economic Report of the President, January 1991* (Washington, DC: U.S. Government Printing Office, 1991), 322.

44. David Leonhardt, "Bush's Record on Jobs," *New York Times,* July 3, 2003.

45. *America's New Beginning: A Program for Economic Recovery* (Washington, DC: White House, 1981), 10. See also Edward Cowan, "Economists at Tax Hearing in House Split on Cuts," *New York Times,* May 3, 1981.

46. Charles L. Schultze, *Memos to the President: A Guide Through Macroeconomics for the Busy Policymaker* (Washington, DC: Brookings Institution Press, 1992), 259; Paul Krugman, *Peddling Prosperity: Economic Sense and Nonsense in the Age of Diminished Expectations* (New York: W.W. Norton, 1994), 262.

47. Andrew Dean, Martin Durand, John Fallon, and Peter Hoeller, "Saving Trends and Behavior in OECD Countries," *OECD Economic Studies* 14 (Spring 1990): 9.

48. Leonard Silk, "Behind the Gloom of Consumers," *New York Times,* November 29, 1991.

49. George Will, "The Threat of Inflation," *Houston Chronicle,* May 23, 1999.

50. Cannon, *President Reagan,* 278.

51. Cited by Jonathan Fuerbringer, "Volcker Says Fed to Continue Tight Money Stand," *New York Times,* February 11, 1982.

52. Albert Rees, *Striking a Balance: Making National Economic Policy* (Chicago: University of Chicago Press, 1984), 71.

53. Paul Craig Roberts, "Is a Depression Brewing?" *Wall Street Journal,* March 3, 1982.

54. Milton Friedman, "The Federal Reserve and Monetary Instability," *Wall Street Journal,* February 1, 1982.

55. Paul Volcker and Toyoo Gyohten, *Changing Fortunes: The World's Money and the Threat to American Leadership* (New York: Random House, 1992), 175.

56. Quoted in Kenneth Bacon, "Is a Depression Brewing?" *Wall Street Journal,* April 19, 1982.

57. Alexander Hommer, "Dow Soars by 38.81," *New York Times,* August 18, 1982.

58. James E. Alt, "Leaning into the Wind or Ducking Out of the Storm? U.S. Monetary Policy in the 1980s," in *Politics and Economics in the Eighties,* ed. Alberto Alesina and Geoffrey Carliner (Chicago: University of Chicago Press, 1991), 46.

59. Alfred L. Malabre, *Lost Prophets: An Insider's History of Modern Economists* (Cambridge: Harvard Business School Press, 1994), 163.

60. Benjamin Friedman, "Comment," in *Politics and Economics in the Eighties,* ed. Alesina and Geoffrey Carliner (Chicago: University of Chicago Press, 1991), 82–83.

61. Arthur Schlesinger Jr., "American Politics on a Darkling Plain," *Wall Street Journal,* March 16, 1982.

62. James Tobin, "How to Think About the Deficit," *New York Review of Books,* September 25, 1986, 44.

63. Quoted by Robert Rubin, *In an Uncertain World: Tough Choices from Wall Street to Washington* (New York: Random House, 2003), 125. See also Bill Clinton, *My Life* (New York: Alfred A. Knopf, 2004), 537.

64. Rubin, *In an Uncertain World,* 356.

65. Paul Krugman, "The Dishonest Truth," *New York Times,* February 23, 2000; Richard Stevenson, "Reaganomics vs. Clintonomics Is a Central Issue in 2000," *New York Times,* February 8, 2000.

66. Ron Suskind, *The Price of Loyalty: George W. Bush, the White House, and the Education of Paul O'Neill* (New York: Simon and Schuster, 2004), 291.

67. Dennis S. Ippolito, "Tax Policy and Spending Policy," *American Politics Quarterly* 19 (October 1991): 463.

68. Robert Pear, "Rich Got Richer in 80s," *New York Times,* January 11, 1991.

69. Andrew Hacker, "The Rich: Who They Are," *New York Times Magazine,* November 19, 1995, 70. See also Keith Brasher, "Gap in Wealth in U.S. Called Widest in West," *New York Times,* April 17, 1995; Edward N. Wolff, *Top Heavy: A Study of Increasing Inequality of Wealth in America* (New York: Twentieth Century Fund Press, 1995), 7.

70. Michael Lewis, "The Rich," *New York Times Magazine,* November 19, 1995.

71. Sylvia Nasar, "The Rich Get Richer," *New York Times,* August 16, 1992.

72. Sylvia Nasar, "Fed Report Gives New Data on Gains by Richest in 80s," *New York Times,* April 21, 1992. See also James T. Patterson, *Restless Giant: The United States from Watergate to Bush v. Gore* (New York: Oxford University Press, 2005), 351–352.

73. Walter Williams, *Reaganism and the Death of Representative Democracy* (Washington, DC: Georgetown University Press, 2003), 9–10.

Chapter 3

1. Dinesh D'Souza, *Ronald Reagan: How an Ordinary Man Became an Extraordinary Leader* (New York: Free Press, 1997), 245.

2. Peggy Noonan, *When Character Was King: A Story of Ronald Reagan* (New York: Viking, 2003), 248–249.

3. Edwin Meese III. *With Reagan: The Inside Story* (Washington, DC: Regnery, 1992), 51.

4. Anne Edwards, *Early Reagan* (New York: William Morrow, 1987), 54.

5. Kiron K. Skinner, Annelise Anderson, and Martin Anderson, eds., *Reagan: A Life in Letters* (New York: Free Press, 2003), 337–338.

6. Edwards, *Early Reagan,* 53.

7. Edmund Morris, *Dutch* (New York: Random House, 1999), 90.

8. Morris, *Dutch,* 89.

9. Mark Shields, "Reagan Had Sympathy but Little Empathy," Creator's Syndicate, June 16, 2004.

10. Skinner, Anderson, and Anderson, *Reagan,* 335.

11. Skinner, Anderson, and Anderson, *Reagan,* 337–338.

12. Robert Dallek, *Ronald Reagan: The Politics of Symbolism* (Cambridge: Harvard University Press, 1984), 34.

13. Jeremy D. Mayer, *Running on Race: Racial Politics in Presidential Campaigns, 1960–2000* (New York: Random House, 2002), 165; "Political News Summary," May 22, 1968, Hubert Humphrey Papers, Minnesota Historical Society.

14. Mayer, *Running on Race,* 164–165.

15. In one speech in the 1970s, he referred to a young black man as "young buck," which was seen as a racially derogatory reference to a young black male. Reagan pleaded ignorance of the term's offensive tone and apologized.

16. Mayer, *Running on Race,* 155.

17. Mayer, *Running on Race,* 153.

18. Mayer, *Running on Race,* 153

19. Mayer, *Running on Race,* 82.

20. Mayer, *Running on Race,* 82.

21. Mayer, *Running on Race,* 153.

22. Malcolm D. MacDougall, *We Almost Made It* (New York: Crown, 1977), 48.

23. "Test of Governor Ronald Reagan's Nationwide Television Address, NBC," March 31, 1976, 1976 Campaign Files, Gerald Ford Library; "Reagan and Busing," no author, no date, 1976 Campaign Files, Gerald Ford Library.

24. Mayer, *Running on Race,* 135.

25. Mayer, *Running on Race,* 134.

26. Mayer, *Running on Race,* 136.

27. Lou Cannon, *President Reagan: The Role of a Lifetime* (New York: Simon and Schuster, 1991), 518–519.

28. Mayer, *Running on Race,* 134.

29. Mayer, *Running on Race,* 134.

30. Author interview with Richard Bond, September 6, 2000; author interview with Doug Bailey, November 13, 2000; author interview with Richard Wirthlin, November 20, 2000.

31. Mayer, *Running on Race,* 154.

32. Wirthlin interview.

33. Mayer, *Running on Race,* 164–165.

34. Mayer, *Running on Race,* 158.

35. Mayer, *Running on Race,* 169–170.

36. Wirthlin interview.

37. Mayer, *Running on Race,* 194.

38. Skinner, Anderson, and Anderson, *Reagan,* 208.

39. Stephen L. Carter, *Reflections of an Affirmative Action Baby* (New York: Basic Books, 1991), 155.

40. Mayer, *Running on Race,* 175.

41. Carter, *Reflections of an Affirmative Action Baby,* 157.

42. Dallek, *Ronald Reagan,* 80.

43. Dallek, *Ronald Reagan,* 81.

44. Mayer, *Running on Race,* 177.

45. Mayer, *Running on Race,* 153.

46. Skinner, Anderson, and Anderson, *Reagan,* 634.

47. Mayer, *Running on Race,* 176.

48. Edwin L. Harper to Ronald Reagan, March 5, 1983, Ronald Reagan Presidential Library.

49. Dallek, *Ronald Reagan,* 82.

50. Jerry Falwell to Ronald Reagan, March 15, 1983, Ronald Reagan Presidential Library.

51. Mayer, *Running on Race,* 202.

52. Stephen R. Graubard, *Command of Office* (New York: Basic Books, 2004).

Chapter 4

1. Peggy Noonan, *When Character Was King: A Story of Ronald Reagan* (New York: Viking, 2001), 14, 325.

2. "Character," WordReference.com Dictionary, www.wordreference.com/definition/character.

3. Dinesh D'Souza, *Ronald Reagan: How an Ordinary Man Became an Extraordinary Leader* (New York: Free Press, 1997), 259.

4. Billy Graham, *Just As I Am: The Autobiography of Billy Graham* (New York: HarperCollins, 1997), 589–590.

5. Jimmy Carter, *Living Faith* (New York: Three Rivers Press, 1998).

6. Paul Kengor, *God and Ronald Reagan: A Spiritual Life* (New York: Regan Books, 2004), ii.

7. Kengor, *God and Ronald Reagan,* x.

8. Jimmy Carter, *Turning Point: A Candidate, a State, and a Nation Come of Age* (New York: Times Books, 1992), 21–27.

9. As cited in Gaddis Smith, *Morality, Reason, and Power: American Diplomacy in the Carter Years* (New York: Hill and Wang, 1986), 28.

10. Douglas Brinkley, *The Unfinished Presidency: Jimmy Carter's Journey Beyond the White House* (New York: Viking, 1998).

11. Brinkley, *Unfinished Presidency,* 412–436.

12. *Boston Globe Magazine,* April 12, 1990.

13. Brinkley, *Unfinished Presidency,* xvi–xvii.

14. Steven F. Hayward, *The Real Jimmy Carter: How Our Worst Ex-President Undermines American Foreign Policy, Coddles Dictators, and Created the Party of Clinton and Kerry* (Lanham, MD: Regnery, 2004), 2, 195.

15. Peggy Noonan, *What I Saw at the Revolution: A Political Life in the Reagan Era* (New York: Random House, 1990), 166.

16. Noonan, *When Character Was King,* 100.

17. D'Souza, *Ronald Reagan,* 212.

18. Lou Cannon, *Governor Reagan: His Rise to Power* (New York: Public Affairs, 2003), 208–209.

19. Cannon, *Governor Reagan,* 211–212.

20. Cannon, *Governor Reagan,* 212–214.

21. Cannon, *Governor Reagan,* 214. Kiron K. Skinner, Annelise Anderson, and Martin Anderson, eds., *Reagan, In His Own Hand: The Writings of Ronald Reagan That Reveal His Revolutionary Vision for America* (New York: Free Press, 2001), 222.

22. Cannon, *Governor Reagan,* 214.

23. Donald T. Critchlow, "Mobilizing Women: The 'Social Issues,'" in *The Reagan Presidency: Pragmatic Conservatism and Its Legacies,* ed. W. Elliot Brownlee and Hugh Davis Graham (Lawrence: University Press of Kansas, 2003), 300.

24. Lou Cannon, *President Reagan: The Role of a Lifetime* (New York: Simon and Schuster, 1991), 804; Critchlow, "Mobilizing Women," 306.

25. Kiron K. Skinner, Annelise Anderson, and Martin Anderson, eds., *Reagan: A Life in Letters* (New York: Free Press, 2003), 364.

26. Ronald Reagan, *An American Life* (New York: Simon and Schuster, 1990), 280.

27. David M. O'Brien, "Federal Judgeships in Retrospect," in *Reagan Presidency,* Brownlee and Graham, 345.

28. O'Brien, "Federal Judgeships in Retrospect," 347–348.

29. Cannon, *President Reagan,* 808.

30. Edwin Meese III, *With Reagan: The Inside Story* (Washington, DC: Regnery 1992), 321.

31. Bork considered *Roe* "an unconstitutional decision, a serious and wholly unjustifiable judicial usurpation of state legislative authority." As cited in Ethan Bonner, *Battle for Justice: How the Bork Nomination Shook America* (New York: W.W. Norton, 1989), 92.

32. Cannon, *President Reagan,* 812.

33. William E. Pemberton, *Exit with Honor: The Life and Presidency of Ronald Reagan* (Armonk, NY: M.E. Sharpe, 1997), 137.

34. Donald T. Regan, *For the Record: From Wall Street to Washington* (New York: Harcourt Brace Jovanovich, 1988), 77.

35. Patrick J. Buchanan, *Right from the Beginning* (Boston: Little, Brown, 1988), 356.

36. Nancy Reagan with William Novak, *My Turn: The Memoirs of Nancy Reagan* (New York: Random House, 1989), 177.

37. Pemberton, *Exit with Honor,* 137.

38. Critchlow, "Mobilizing Women," 313.

39. Cannon, *President Reagan,* 590.

40. D'Souza, *Ronald Reagan,* 53.

41. Cannon, *President Reagan,* 59–60.

42. Cannon, *President Reagan,* 487–489.

43. Haynes Johnson, *Sleepwalking Through History: America in the Reagan Years* (New York: W.W. Norton, 1991), 184.

44. Johnson, *Sleepwalking Through History,* 183–184.

45. Johnson, *Sleepwalking Through History,* 183–184.

46. Johnson, *Sleepwalking Through History,* 184.

47. Johnson, *Sleepwalking Through History,* 184–185.

48. Cannon, *President Reagan,* 801.

49. Cannon, *President Reagan,* 795.

50. Cannon, *President Reagan,* 800–801.

51. Pemberton, *Exit with Honor,* 146.

52. Cannon, *President Reagan,* 801–802.

53. Johnson, *Sleepwalking Through History,* 185.

54. *Cannon, President Reagan,* 802.

55. Johnson, *Sleepwalking Through History,* 185.

56. Wilbur Edel, *The Reagan Presidency: An Actor's Finest Performance* (New York: Hippocrene Books, 1992), 296.

57. Peter J. Wallison, *Ronald Reagan: The Power of Conviction and the Success of His Presidency* (Boulder, CO: Westview Press, 2003), 168–169.

58. Elliott Abrams, *Undue Process: A Story of How Political Differences Are Turned Into Crimes* (New York: Free Press, 1993).

59. Noonan, *When Character Was King,* 279.

60. As cited in Michael Schaller, *Reckoning with Reagan: America and Its President in the 1980s* (New York: Oxford University Press, 1992), 155–156.

61. Kyle Longley, *In the Eagle's Shadow: The United States and Latin America* (Wheeling, IL: Harlan Davidson, 2002), 288–291.

62. Cannon, *President Reagan,* 385.

63. As cited in Lawrence E. Walsh, *Firewall: The Iran-Contra Conspiracy and Cover-Up* (New York: W.W. Norton, 1997), 4.

64. William S. Cohen and George J. Mitchell, *Men of Zeal: A Candid Inside Story of the Iran-Contra Hearings* (New York: Viking, 1988), xx.

65. Robert C. McFarlane with Zofia Smardz, *Special Trust* (New York: Cadell and Davis, 1994), 31.

66. McFarlane, *Special Trust,* 34.

67. Pemberton, *Exit with Honor,* 181–183.

68. Cannon, *President Reagan,* 638.

69. Cannon, *President Reagan,* 683.

70. Cannon, *President Reagan,* 689–690.

71. Cannon, *President Reagan,* 702.

72. Pemberton, *Exit with Honor,* 188.

73. Cannon, *President Reagan*, 708–709.

74. Cannon, *President Reagan*, 710–711.

75. Cannon, *President Reagan*, 712.

76. Cannon, *Governor Reagan*, 103–105.

77. Anne Edwards, *Early Reagan* (New York: William Morrow, 1987), 439.

78. Cannon, *President Reagan*, 713.

79. Cannon, *President Reagan*, 711.

80. As cited in Schaller, *Reckoning with Reagan*, 154.

81. As cited in Cannon, *President Reagan*, 714.

82. As cited in Cannon, *President Reagan*, 653.

83. As cited in Cannon, *President Reagan*, 738.

84. As cited in Pemberton, *Exit with Honor*, 191.

85. As cited in Pemberton, *Exit with Honor*, 191–192.

86. As cited in Noonan, *When Character Was King*, 272–273.

87. Martin Anderson, *Revolution: The Reagan Legacy* (Stanford, CA: Hoover Institution Press, 1990), 289–291.

88. *New York Times*, January 26, 2003.

Epilogue

1. *New York Times*, January 26, 2003.

2. *Wall Street Journal*, June 9, 2004.

3. *New York Times*, January 26, 2003.

4. *New York Times*, January 26, 2003.

5. Howard Fineman, "How Reagan's Passing Helps Bush: It's Easier Now to Invoke Aura of an Icon—and It's Very Safe," June 7, 2004, MSNBC.com, www.msnbc.msn.com/id/5164981/site/newsweek.

6. Ronald Reagan Jr., "Ron Reagan Jr.'s Eulogy for Ronald Reagan," June 14, 2004, NewsMax.com, www.newsmax.com/archives/articles/2004/6/14/125156.shtml.

7. David Talbot, "Reagan Blasts Bush," August 14, 2003, Salon.com, www.salon.com/news/feature/2003/04/14/ron_reagan/index_np.html. Reagan added that his mother shared his "distrust of some of these [Bush] people. She gets that they're trouble in all kinds of ways. She doesn't like their religious fervor, their aggression."

8. Ron Reagan, "The Case Against George W. Bush," *Esquire*, September 2004, 56, 57.

9. Patrick J. Buchanan, *Where the Right Went Wrong: How Neoconservatives Subverted the Reagan Revolution and Hijacked the Bush Presidency* (New York: Thomas Dunne Books, 2004), 6, 9.

10. Jonah Goldberg, "George W. Bush, Preservative: Has Government Become the Answer?" *National Review Online*, January 21, 2004, www.nationalreview.com/goldberg/goldberg200401211053.asp.

11. Goldberg, "George W. Bush, Preservative."

12. *New York Times*, January 26, 2003.

13. *Washington Post*, June 11, 2004.

About the Authors

Kyle Longley is the Snell Family Dean's Distinguished Professor of history at Arizona State University. His works include *Senator Albert A. Gore Sr.: Tennessee Maverick*; *In the Eagle's Shadow: The United States and Latin America*; and *The Sparrow and the Hawk: Costa Rica and the United States During the Rise of Jose Figueres*.

Jeremy D. Mayer is an associate professor at the George Mason School of Public Policy. He specializes in presidential elections, public opinion, racial politics, and foreign policy. He has published widely on American politics and his book *Running on Race: Racial Politics in Presidential Campaigns 1960–2000* was selected by *Washington Monthly* as one of the best political books of 2002. He is the author of the forthcoming *Wired Politics: Journalism and Governance*.

Michael Schaller is Regent's Professor of History at the University of Arizona. His research interests include twentieth-century United States, foreign policy, and the United States and Asia. Among his many books are *Right Turn: American Life in the Reagan-Bush Era 1980–1992*; *Present Tense: The United States Since 1945*, with Robert D. Schulzinger and Karen Anderson; *The United States and China: Into the Twentieth-first Century*; *Douglas MacArthur: The Far Eastern General*; and *Altered States: The United States and Japan Since the Occupation*.

John W. Sloan is a professor of political science at the University of Houston. He has conducted research at several presidential libraries and written books on the Eisenhower and Reagan presidencies. Among his books are *The Reagan Effect: Economics and Presidential Leadership*; *Eisenhower and the Management of Prosperity*; and *Public Policy in Latin America: A Comparative Study*.

Index